FARM RAISED

Rusty Moore

Table of Contents

Farm Raised

While writing these stories, my mind would wander back to those days on our little farm in rural eastern Kentucky, where I grew up. It was a small farm, just over nine acres, but the farm provided my family with rural living and a wonderful place to grow up. The work was hard and never-ending, though looking back on those days, I'm thankful for each day and each lesson I learned as that has carried me through my life, and I use those lessons even today. I call on those lessons to make decisions and help me guide my children into their lives.

As I write each one of the memories down, I'm reminded of all the sensory memories as well. Like the smell of mom's cornbread in the oven, she made cornbread every day for supper. The smell of bean and corn blossoms in late spring as the plants matured. Even the different smells of manure as we cleaned out the barn or the chicken house, the sour, pungent smell of the hog pens lofting through the holler in the dog days of summer. The smell of hay drying in the fields or the fresh, turned soil in the early spring as Mr. McGuire plowed our garden for planting. Those smells still linger in my mind today, along with many more, and enjoying these memories with the smells and sounds bring great pleasure as I walk back through those days of my childhood.

Memories of my mother are the very best of these memories. The way she never seemed to stop working, there was always something that needed to be done. She would stop in time to get ready for church though, every Wednesday night, Sunday morning Sunday School, and Sunday night church service, my mother was there for them all. The quiet wisdom mom would share with me when I needed it and even when I didn't know I needed it is a cherished part of my life that I often call upon today. I can still hear her sweet voice guiding me through life.

Hay Fever

The morning seemed to start out hot as I started my chores. Right now, that was feeding the hogs and milking the cow dad picked for me to milk. As daylight broke, I knew what the day held, and I was dreading it. I had been through this day many times before in my short twelve-year life span. The day would go like this. Up before dawn to get the feeding chores done and get the cows milked and turned out. I would feed the hogs as soon as it was light enough for them to see. My little brother Randy would feed the chickens before dawn broke so the food would be out when they came off the roost. Mom would have breakfast ready by the time we were done with the animals. We would eat a hearty breakfast of bacon, sausage, eggs, and biscuits and gravy, then spend a few minutes resting at the kitchen table while Dad smoked another cigarette and drank another cup of coffee.

Dad would tell us what we needed to go pick from the garden before the dew rose. This was also his way of telling mom what he wanted for dinner.

"Get your mom some green beans, corn and dig her some taters." He'd say as the smoke came out of his mouth in what we thought were word puffs. Mom would smile as we went outside to gather what would be our supper tonight. If we wanted something added, all we had to do was pick it and mom would cook it. Like fried green tomatoes or lettuce and onions wilted with bacon grease. After gathering the vegetables and setting them on the back porch we would go back in to see what else we needed to do.

"Alright, boys get the water ready," Dad would say.

3

Me and my younger brother knew what that meant. We would grab the two big water jugs and head to the pump house where the big freezer was. In that freezer, our parents kept all our meat from a butchered hog every spring and fall and a beef steer every fall. The reason we were standing on stools was to let us reach in and grab two of several old plastic milk jugs dad had cut the top off of and filled with water to make big ice blocks. One block in each water jug then we used the garden hose to fill up the water jugs and refill the plastic jugs dad had turned into an ice maker and return it to the freezer.

While we were in the pump house, we would grab an old Prince Albert tobacco can and stuff it in one of our pockets. Inside the can were a two pieces of fishing line and a few small fishing hooks. I carried one water jug, and my brother carried the other one. We would meet dad in the barn. In the barn, there was a nineteen seventy-one, yellow long, wheelbase ford pickup truck. This truck was dad's work horse. It hauled everything from our groceries once a month to cow manure in the spring for the garden. Dad would be loading the pitchforks, and ropes and checking the wood racks he had built to raise the level of hay we could stack onto the truck. Once he was satisfied, we would climb up into the cab and head to the hay field.

The hayfield was about five acres of bottomland owned by Mr. Douglas, a business owner from Ashland. It had a large barn standing on it where Mr. Douglas kept two old cars, and there was a small lake with a dock to cast our fishing line from. Dad maintained the open grass area for the hay it produced; we had to cut the hay twice a summer, this was the first cut.

Our neighbor Mr. McGuire and dad had worked out a deal for Mr. McGuire to cut and bail the hay for some of the bails. There was always a strip of hay along the outside of the field where the ground was too rough to take the bailer. That is where we would begin our work as the dew was rising. Dad would lay the rope out. It laid over the cab and down into the center of the bed of the truck out onto the open tailgate where it would hang down to the ground. After we loaded all the hay onto the truck dad would tie the ends together and back the loaded truck into the barn. We would hook a manual lever action pulley, we called the red dog, to the rope and to the rafter of the barn. Dad would simply drive the truck out from under a load of hay, and we could put it away later. In the hayfield, dad would drive the truck along as I and my brother would rake the hay and throw it up in the truck. We worked all the way around the field like this. After we had picked up all the loose hay dad would tie the two ends of the rope together and turn to me and my brother.

"Ya'll want to ride back or see if the fish are biting?" Dad would always ask us as if the answer would ever be any different. My brother would jump up into the cab and grab our Prince Albert can, and we would run as fast as we could to the lake. Cut a long willow branch, tie our lines and hook on and look for bait. The most readily available bait was Japanize beetles, or that's what we called them; they were all over the willow trees around the lake. We would fish as hard and fast as we could because we knew when dad came back with our older brother and his friends the real work would start.

About an hour later, though it seemed like a couple of minutes for us, we would see dad in the old yellow Ford pickup coming down the gravel lane into the hay field. Usually, our brother would be following him in his cheville along with his friends. We knew not to keep dad waiting, so we cut our lines off and stuffed them back into the Prince Albert can, and headed to the truck. The dew was gone, and the day felt very hot and dry, the only type of day to put up hay.

My younger brother was too little to throw the bales up into the bed of the truck, so he would get in the bed of the truck and stack the bales as they came flying in. The rest of us would throw the bales up into the bed of the truck as the truck rolled slowly along with my dad at the wheel. Once the stack got too high for me to throw the haybale up, my job would be to run out ahead and line the haybales up or jump up and help my little brother with the stack. We would continue this process until we had two rows above the cab. The hay was stacked in a crisscross pattern, with each layer tying the one below it down. My older brother would climb up and tie the load down with the rope for extra security and we would sit on top of the load as we went back to the farm. The wind blowing on us during the several mile drive back to our farm was a welcome relief to cool us down and dry the sweat.

Back at the barn dad would back the truck into the barn so we could unload the hay into its holding place. The barn was completely closed in. There were no windows or vents, just opened doors at each end. This made the unloading much hotter and dustier. We all would take turns stacking the hay into the barn till we could hardly breathe then, someone else would take our place so we could catch our breath and get a drink of water. The only good thing about unloading was that it went fast because we were all trying to get out of that barn as fast as possible.

Dad would pull the truck out of the barn, and we would all climb into the back and head back to the hayfield. The loose straw, dust, and debris from the load would swirl up as the truck got up to speed, it made me think this must be what it's like to be in a tornado. Back at the hay field we would start where we left off and load another load.

After unloading the second load mom would be standing outside by the lane with our lunch dad would slow the truck down and mom would hand us a carboard box with several bologna and cheese sandwiches and a can of Pepsi for each of us. At the hay field dad would pull the truck into a shady spot and we would all get to eat lunch, and rest for a few minutes.

As we pulled back out to start another load of hay, I saw my older brother and my dad whispering. I didn't realize this summer would be a milestone for me.

"Sure, he can" my brother said as he smiled at me. My dad turned to me and motioned at me with his finger. I went up to him not knowing what was going on.

"Think you can drive the truck?" Dad said with a smile.

"Yes, sir." I said with as much confidence as I could muster up.

My twelve-year-old self suddenly was bursting with confidence and excitement. I climbed into that old truck and started her up without even looking at my father. I had driven the truck a few times at the farm in the pastures, but only short little trips simply moving the truck from one spot to another. This time I would be driving for real even if I never got the truck out of bulldog gear.

I had to sit way up on the steering wheel so my feet could push the clutch all the way in. I revved the engine a little and slowly let out the clutch as the truck started moving ever so slowly. I felt like I was in charge of the day now and was smiling the biggest smile of my life.

We continued around the hay field until the truck was loaded for a third time, tied it all off, and headed for the barn.

There were only a few bails left for the last trip so my dad let my older brother and his buddies go, me and my younger brother could handle the rest. I knew from experience that after we got this last partial load into the barn the work would continue until we had done the evening feeding and milking, and night fell. Sleep and rest were a welcome friend at night, and no matter how tired we were we were always excited to see what the next day would bring.

A Summer Monster

I thought I was in trouble the way my father came in noisily through the back door that morning, before dawn. He was still carrying the slop bucket he used to feed the hogs, and he had an unusually worried look on his face. His knuckles were white, showing the grip he had on that slop bucket as the smell of rotten food began to make its way around the kitchen.

"You boys ain't to go outside till it gets daylight!" he said. My younger brother and I knew he meant what he said by the tone in his voice. So, we didn't question his orders. Besides, it just meant more time to kill before we had to head outside and do our chores.

"I've never seen anything like it." He said, heading across the kitchen to the coffee percolator, still holding that slop bucket. My brother and I just sat there, wanting him to tell us what he had seen, but we were afraid to ask. We had never seen him like this.

Finally, he sat that bucket down, poured himself a cup of coffee, and began.

"That thing was so black I could see it in the dark. Just seeing it made chills run from my head to my toes. The way you feel when a snake surprises you. Its eyes changed colors; they went from red to purple to green and then back to red with no light shining on them. It… it seemed to float across the yard between the barn and the house. I threw the other slop bucket at it, and it went right through it. Then, it floated out of sight like a puff of black mist and was gone." Dad finished talking as he sat down.

I didn't notice until he went to light a cigarette that his hands were shaking. I had only seen his hands shaking one other time in my young life. That was when my little sister had pneumonia and was unconscious. He knelt beside the couch where she was laying and prayed. His hands were trembling as he wiped tears from his eyes.

Even with him so upset and the scarry description of the black thing. Which was what it came to be called whenever the subject came up. My little brother and I had been raised not to be afraid of the dark or anything in it. Therefore, it was hard for us to be afraid of something we hadn't even seen. So that morning after daybreak, we went outside and looked at the spot where Dad said he had seen it. There was nothing there but that old slop bucket lying in the wet morning dew on the grass. We pretty much dismissed it. In fact, the only time it came up was when one of us would have to go outside after dark for something.

My brother would start with. "You better watch out for the black thing. Don't look at its eyes." Things of that nature the way kids do. Which I must say seemed to infuriate my father. He never said anything, though, as if he knew we would get ours.

As the summer wore on, we started our usual camping trips in the woods around our little farm here in Kentucky. The black thing had faded into a distant memory, even for my father. It was on one of those camping trips, however, that my brother and I got ours.

The trip started as so many did back then. The other boys, my cousins, would show up, and we would start playing an outside game like S.W.A.T., football, or baseball. As the evening came on, though, we would pack up our limited and, by today's standards, crude camping gear and head off into the woods.

My family always raised a big garden and had lots of chickens, so the food for the night was never a problem. Half of the group would go into the garden and pick corn, tomatoes, and potatoes and whatever else suited their fancy. The other half would have to wait till after dark, then sneak into the chicken house and grab a hen by the feet and neck at the same time so it couldn't squawk or start flapping around, which would stir the other chickens and our father. We had plenty of chickens but that didn't give us any right to take even one of them. On this particular night, though, we made it without any problems from the chickens. We were in our usual camping spot, in a small grove of oak trees at the corner of our property, and after gathering firewood and picking places to sit and eventually lay down, we built the fire and settled in for the night. The night began as usual with someone telling a lie about some girl they had gotten close to at school and passing around the stolen cigarettes from our father's dresser drawers. There were six of us on that fateful night. Myself, my little brother Randy, and our four cousins Mark, Bones, Keith, and Jeff. Randy and I had our usual equipments: an old blanket each, a hatchet, two dented and scratched canteens, one flashlight, and two books of matches.

"These were the most important," my father used to say. The other boys had their usual stuff: backpacks, knives, lanterns, and sleeping bags. My cousin Bones always seemed to have food stuffed into everything he could get it into. Once we were settled into camp, with a fire going, we began to talk about the things teenage boys talked about back then. Girls, cars, hunting, fishing, always cussing because we could without our parents there.

It was about eleven o'clock when Bones let the rest of us know we had drunk all the water. We kept it in a plastic milk jug we had washed out for camping trips. After some discussion and deliberation, some threats and name-calling. It was decided that Keith and Jeff would go after some water. They had to walk in the dark back to my parents' house, where they could fill the jugs from the hose outside the house. They took two of the flashlights and headed off into the darkness. As they disappeared down the hill into the darkness of the valley where our house stood, my little brother shouted.

"Watch out for the black thing!" We all laughed, we could even hear Keith and Jeff laughing in the distance.

Several minutes later, we could hear the thud of footsteps and the wheeze of heavy breathing. We could hear the brush and sapling trees being pushed aside as someone or something came towards our camp at a dead run. We suddenly found ourselves scrambling for anything that could be used as a weapon. I grabbed my pocketknife and flipped open the largest blade. Then, I took a moment to check on my little brother. He had grabbed a piece of an oak limb that was waiting to be burned. We looked at each other and gave a small nod of assurance. Mark had pulled out the bayonet someone had given him. Bones just stood there with his mouth hanging open, but we knew if it came down to it, he would be there for us. As Randy took a baseball hitter's stance, Keith and Jeff came blasting back into camp. Dropping the jugs they had taken to refill and falling to their knees, out of breath from their run back up the hill.

"What's going on?" Mark asked, almost demanding an answer with the tone of his voice. Jeff held up his hand, signaling to wait a moment till they caught their breath.

After several minutes, they finally began to tell us what had happened.

"The black thing," Keith began.

"We seen it" he seemed so earnest with his statement.

Me and the other boys just stood there, we couldn't believe what we were hearing. The sudden realization that we were outside and the black thing had been seen was starting to grip us all.

"You guys know that I don't lie, ever," Jeff said. Then, he began to describe what he had seen.

"It was blacker than night. I mean, we could see it without our lights, and if we shined our lights on it, it disappeared. Its eyes turned color, and it floated across the ground just like your dad said.

"Boys, I'm scared, and I don't care who knows it." Jeff was staring at each of us as he was speaking. This meant something to us as Keith and Jeff were older than us by two years. We all sat in silence around the now bigger than normal campfire. Each of us had to put this in its our own perspective so we could deal with being out there in the dark.

What seemed like an hour or so passed with very little being said; I don't recall anything, as I remember we just sat there looking from one to another, hoping someone would have a good response and know what to do.

"But what are you going to do about the water?" Bones said.

We all looked at each other, knowing we had to do something.

"Where did you see it?" I asked.

"Down by the gate that leads into the yard," Keith said.

A few more minutes passed in silence as we all just stared into the fire.

"Come on Mark, let's go get the water," I said, thinking to myself that somehow, I wanted to see this thing.

Mark looked at me as if I had asked him to give me a lung or something. Somehow, I knew I had to go down that hill and face this thing. After several attempts at prodding and explaining that it was probably gone by now and letting him know what giant chicken he was if he didn't go, he agreed.

We started down the hill very slowly, checking the whole area in front of us before taking each step. After several minutes, we made it down to the creek without seeing anything. So, our senses had settled down and we weren't being as thorough as we had been in the beginning. I was in front, leading us down the narrow cow path that ran between the fence and the creek.

"I bet they were just goofing around and trying to scare us," Mark whispered as we came to the end of the path.

I came to the familiar water gate our dad had built. It marked the spot where the small creek came from our neighbor's land to our land under the fence. Dad had built the gate to hang down from the posts so it could be lifted by flood water instead of losing the whole fence. It was there I froze in my tracks, unable to speak, hardly able to breathe. I slowly turned toward Mark to show him the terror that had frozen me. I didn't need to show him anything. He had seen it on his own and was fighting his own paralysis.

"What is that?" I finally managed to utter.

And although I knew exactly what it was, I still waited for and wanted an answer. It was everything those who had seen it before said it was. You could really see it in the dark with no light on it. In fact, if you shined a light on it, it disappeared. After several minutes that seemed like days, the black thing began to float down the little creek. It was then Mark and I regained our wits and began to follow it. It was a few feet out in front of us when it turned suddenly and floated across the small pool of water in the creek.

"Run" was all I heard, and to this day, I don't know if Mark or I spoke that word or I did because we both heard it, but neither of us can remember saying it. After a quick hundred-yard sprint to the gate that led through the fence into the yard, the spot where Keith and Jeff said they saw it. We were over the gate in seconds and standing on the back porch, where we felt safe.

Minutes passed in silence, I was trying franticly to put a name or explanation to this thing. To reason it into something my mind could handle.

Had it floated? Of course, it had and over water too. Even the most graceful of animals bounce, bob, or in some way show their feet touching the ground. But this thing floated like wood smoke on a cold, wet morning. What kind of animal or thing could do that?

"Where's the hose to fill the jug?" Mark asked as if nothing had happened. I jerked back to reality as Mark finished his question. Mark looked at me as if to say just forget about it and pretend we never saw it. But I knew we had seen it, and we would have to go back through that pasture after we filled this jug.

We filled the jug and left the porch unceremoniously and without speaking about what we had seen or what we were about to do. This time, we opened the gate and walked slowly through. My father would have been proud, I thought, as we always jumped or climbed it.

"I've got it," Mark declared.

"We will keep our lights on and swinging in front of us. If the lights are on it, we can't or won't see it, right?" he asked as he swung his flashlight back and forth in front of us.

Better than any plan I had at the time, so we decided to go with it.

"You lead this time," I said as firmly as I could.

"No way, I'll stay behind you and carry the water," Mark said taking the water jug out of my hand and shuffling in behind me.

At the end of our garden was what we called the hallway. It was a strip of land about eight feet wide. It ran the width of our garden on one side with our property border fence on the other side. There was a small pool of water in the creek on this side of the hallway. It was there that I saw the black thing again. It was on the far side of the creek, just standing or floating or something. Mark never spoke a word as he ran past me carrying the jug of water. As for me, I just stood there watching this thing. It slowly floated out to the middle of the pool of water, turned, and started floating upstream. I watched it as far as I could without climbing the fence. I wasn't that interested in following it anyway. I knew somehow that it didn't want to hurt anybody, though I still didn't know what it was. I went back to camp and told the group what I had seen and how I felt about the black thing now. Though it was the end of the mystery for me, the others still feared it and would for years to come.

Dad saw it a few more times that summer, but he didn't seem to be afraid of it either. We never saw it again after the first frost, but for that year, we had a summer monster.

My First Lure

As a kid growing up on a farm in eastern Kentucky in the late sixties and seventies, my life was very rural. If we ate it, we grew it, if we needed it, we made it for the most part. I never really challenged that lifestyle. That also meant that if we were bored, we had to figure out what to do. In the summertime my younger brother and I would decide we were going to go crawdad fishing in the small creek that ran by our house. This operation would take a whole morning or afternoon. First, we would have to go up in the woods to cut a pole to use. It had to be just the right length and diameter, be strong enough to hold up and yet flexible enough to work, and light enough not to wear us out holding it. We called it sour wood, but I'm sure it had an official name; it was hollow inside, which made it lighter than other woods.

It grew in straight lengths and was usually not very thick, giving us the flexibility we needed. Now, to be honest, there was no flexibility or anything else that was needed for this task, but we put our hearts into it anyway; remember we were making up something to do. After we cut our poles, we would head to the pump house and get our fishing line. It was a short length of braided fishing line dad had given us specifically for crawdad fishing. We would unroll it from the stick spool we kept it rolled up on and inspect every inch of it. Then, tie it on the small end of our pole. Next, we needed bait. Red worms were the bait of choice, and we knew all the best places to get those. We grabbed a shovel and a small tin can and headed to the edge of the garden. It usually only took a few digs, and we would have enough. We put the shovel back in its place grabbed our poles and headed for the creek. We would walk up and down, looking down into the clear water, looking for the biggest holes we could find. Once we decided on a place, we would tie a red worm on the end of our fishing lines. We would lay on our stomachs and lower the worm into the mouth of the crawdad holes we would hold the worm there and watch intently as the crawdad would slowly ease out of its hole to grab the worm. As the crawdad would venture out of its lair to take the bait sometimes, I would imagine it was a dragon that I was coaxing out of its cave. I watched as the crawdad would take the worm in its big pinchers and start to move back into its hole. Then, it wouldn't let go even after being lifted out of the water and put into a bucket. My brother would get bored quickly and move on to something else, but I would remain. My dad would sit on the porch and watch us.

"Put those back, so they'll be there for bait when we really go fishing," he would yell from the glider on the porch. The only problem with that was we never went fishing. Dad was always too busy working on the farm.

On other days, we would go and do what I thought of as real fishing for real fish. We would take short lengths of braided fishing lines and small hooks from our dad's tackle box and ride our bikes down the road to where the creek got a little bigger, and we could fish for creek chubs and small sunfish. We would dump our bikes and cut small willow branches sometimes. It took a bit to find the right one. As I looked and looked, the anticipation of fishing would grow inside me till I was so excited I could barely stand it. Whether we were fishing under the roots of a tree or under one of the small bridges, the sun reflected off the clear water, the smell of the creek mud. The sound of the water rippling over the shallow parts was something that I can still smell and hear today. I would sit on the roots of a big sycamore tree where the water had washed out a hole underneath three or four feet deep for hours, catching little, tiny fish.

Those were some of the best days for me, as fishing was so important then and still is today.

As I grew up and began thinking about bigger and better ways to fish, I would ask my dad if we could go. He would always say yes as soon as I get the garden planted or the roof of the chicken house patched, then we'll go. But it rarely came time to go fishing; I can remember only four or five trips with my dad to a creek called East Fork. We went there a few times to catch catfish and sunfish. We only stayed it seemed like a few minutes, though it was probably several hours. Then we always had to come home to do the feeding.

Ross's Lake was a small lake John Ross used to water his black Angus cattle. It was in the holler on the other side of Milton McGuire's ridge. It was across Mr. McGuires fence line, so we weren't allowed to go there. It was also John Rosse's land, and my dad didn't get along with John Ross. I also believe dad, who was not a good swimmer and therefore never taught me or my brother how to swim, was afraid of us going around the lake. This meant that if we got caught over there, we would get the belt in a big way. All of this should have kept me away from the lake, but I loved to fish so much that the thought of the bass in that lake would keep me up at night.

One day, I remember it was raining, so I told mom I was going to my shelter in the woods. Mom rolled her eyes. She knew she wouldn't be able to stop me but thought I was a bit crazy to go out in the rain. I took off up the hill in the opposite direction of Ross's Lake so if dad saw me going, he wouldn't think I was heading that way. I also figured that in the rain, dad would be far less apt to follow me. I went to the top of the ridge and then just over, out of sight of the house. Then my long trek started up and around Terrapin Ridge and then down into John Ross's holler. As I made my way to the edge of the woods just by the lake, I paused as if I were on a mission in some foreign war, and this was the moment of truth. I actually remember sitting and waiting to make sure no one had followed me before I really broke the rules. After what I felt was a long enough time, I slowly walked down to the water. It was as if I were visiting some sacred land and was stepping onto it for the first time.

I was looking all around the lake, remembering the rocks along the edge, the trees on the far side. I could see bluegill and bass swimming away from the edge as I approached; this made my need to go fishing even more pressing. I could see where the cows walked around close to the water, creating a small path all the way around the lake. I was on the upper end of the lake, the shallow end, but I was determined to get to the dam at the other end. I walked as non-saliently as I could, I don't know why. As I walked out onto the damn of that lake, I knew there was no stopping me now; I could do anything I wanted. My next question was, how was I going to catch the bass in this lake? My little bit of stolen fishing line and small hooks would never do here. I knew I had to figure this out, and I started thinking about it as I headed back home, the way I had come, the long way home, in the rain.

One day, later that summer, when we were at the Western Auto store in Catlettsburg, a small town near our home in Kentucky. My brother and I were running up and down the aisles, playing as usual. Then, I came to the fishing section. I froze in my tracks, looking at the hooks, bobbers, and sinkers, the things I saw hanging there were amazing to me; some of them I had no idea what they were or how to use them. Then I saw it, the four-inch black and silver Rapala fishing lure. I had seen it in a copy of Field and Stream magazine I was thumbing through at Foodland while mom was grocery shopping. My mind instantly went into a fantasy world where I was catching bass after bass at Ross's Lake on this amazing fishing lure. I didn't know how I was going to buy it; I didn't even know how the lure worked, let alone how I was going to use it, but somehow, I knew this was the key to Ross's Lake.

My mind was racing on our ride home that day; no one in the car knew what I had found or how important it was to me. I couldn't ask my parents to buy it for me because even if they bought it for me, they would know I was planning a trip to Ross's Lake, and that would not be allowed. I had to figure this out. I had to have that fishing lure.

My brother and I got an allowance each week of thirty-five cents. The lure cost one dollar and seventy cents. Oh boy, I had to do math. This meant I would have to wait five weeks to buy this lure, a big challenge but I was going to do it. So, after I got that first week's allowance and I put it in a small jar I had found, I couldn't wait till the next week. As I watched my little brother spend his allowance on candy at the general store we rode our bikes to I wondered if this was worth it. But then I'd close my eyes and picture myself at the edge of Ross's Lake, catching bass after bass. The summer wore on, and before I knew it, I had saved one dollar and seventy-five cents, more money than I had ever had. Now just to get back to the Western Auto store.

In the summertime, my brother and I would go with our dad to the livestock yard in Catlettsburg. My brother and I would run around looking at all the big bulls or horses, goats, anything that we didn't have on our farm. We went every Tuesday for just a couple of hours to watch the cattlemen bring their livestock in, and on Thursdays, we would stay for the livestock sale. The Western Auto store was about three blocks from the stockyard, and if my dad found out I had left the stockyard and had gone there, he would take his belt to me for sure. It was Tuesday morning and dad was getting us ready to go to the stockyard. I was planning my break to run to the western auto and was willing to take the chance to do it. I counted my money one more time as I nervously put it in my pocket. However, on that particular Tuesday morning mom said she needed to go to Foodland grocery shopping while dad was at the stockyard. Dad agreed and we were off to Catlettsburg. The Western Auto store was next door to Foodland. Once there, I stepped up and, in my bravest voice, told my dad that I would stay with mom and help her. Dad shook his head, mom smiled and closed the door, dad and my little brother drove off.

Once inside Foodland, I asked mom if I could run over to Western Auto for a minute just to look at the fishing stuff. She looked at me puzzled but said go ahead, but hurry right back. I ran as fast as I could to the store, ran inside and went straight back to the fishing stuff. There it was, the four-inch black and silver Rapala. I double-checked the price it was still one dollar and seventy cents. I walked up and placed my new Rapala on the counter, so proud of what I was doing. The man rang it up one dollar and seventy-three cents. I even got change back, and in those days, two cents bought a good handful of candy. I shoved the Rapala and my change into my jeans pocket, pushing it down in there so it couldn't come out. I ran back to Foodland and found mom; I was walking around with my chest sticking out and my greatest possession in the pocket of my jeans.

Now, my brother and I shared everything there were no secrets between us, but I was not going to share this until after I made it to Ross's lake and tried it out for myself. I waited for just the right time to head over to Ross's Lake. I could always go to the woods without question usually, but this time, I had to make sure my little brother didn't follow me. It was late afternoon, and my brother was playing in the match box city. I had been playing there too but said I was bored and had gone inside. As soon as I was inside, I grabbed my Rapala and the ten feet or so of line I had stolen from my dad's tackle box and hidden in my bedroom. I told mom I was going up in the woods as I almost ran out of the house. I had to stay on the other side of the house so my little brother wouldn't see me heading off into the woods. I made it up into Harlan Sparkman's property, then cut straight up into the woods on Mr. McGuire's land. As I walked up the hill, I was looking for the perfect long keen maple pole that I could use for my rod. I found the perfect one, took out my pocket knife and cut it down. I trimmed it as I walked up the hill. After a few minutes, I was at Mr. McGuires' fence line and could see the lake in the holler below.

I looked behind me to make sure no one had followed. As I climbed through the fence, I was so excited I could barely contain it. I ran down the other side of the hill dodging blackberry briars and scrub brush. Finally, I was standing at the edge of Ross's Lake with my four-inch black and silver Rapala. My hands were trembling with excitement as I tied the line to the end of my makeshift fishing rod and then to the Rapala. Now, what I thought as I stood there, ready to fish. I tossed the lure out to the end of the string, and it just sat there floating as I waited for the fish to grab it. I slowly moved the pole and noticed the movement of the lure. I took a couple of steps forward, watching the lure swing back and forth, mimicking the movement of a small minnow. I only took a couple more steps, and wham! A small bass grabbed it. I pulled it onto the bank and grabbed it, holding it up like a gift from the heavens.

"Yes" I screamed, as I held that first bass up, because I knew I had unlocked Ross's lake.

I spent many days after that with my four-inch black and silver Rapala, walking around Ross's lake, catching bass after bass. I even let my little brother in on it and we would spend whole days there catching bass. Although it was fun to share this adventure with my little brother, those days that I was sneaking over there and fishing by myself, feeling like I was on some big adventures, were some of the most exciting days of my young life.

Dad must have followed us at some point because one evening at supper, he said.

"Boys, if you're going to go over to Ross's lake, just promise me you won't get in the water." Well, I had no intention of swimming; for me, it was all about catching bass after bass as I smiled and nodded.

Chasing Rats

On our small farm in rural Kentucky, we had several structures. A house, pump house, barn, and chicken house with an enclosed chicken yard. There were three hog houses. The hay mound, a shed-like structure with vertical wooden planks spaced just wide enough for the cows to get their heads into the hay we filled it with. Pretty normal for a small farm in the nineteen sixties. The barn was a long, narrow structure built with rough-cut oak rafters. The wood had seasoned there in the barn, and it was so hard you could barely drive a nail into it. Inside the barn was a small room that was completely closed in except for the entry door and a small boarded-up opening where we loaded the corn in through. This was the corn crib, and oh, what a room it was.

The room was about fifteen feet by fifteen feet, and the wall went up to the roof of the barn. We had built the floor twice with old tongue and groove boards; the first layer had the boards all lined up in one direction, then a layer of sheet plastic went down, and the next layer of tongue and groove boards had them all lined up perpendicular to the first layer. This was for strength to hold the feed; it would keep the moisture down, and the rats out was the reason our dad gave for doing it this way. The walls were put together with all sizes of boards cut to fit as tightly as possible. Dad's brother, Uncle Fred, had a paper route. That's the only job I ever knew he had. He had a Volkswagen Rabbit and would deliver papers every day. He had told my dad about the thin aluminum sheets they used for printing the paper and how they discarded them after using them. Dad went to the Ashland Daily Independent and came back with a pickup truckload of these aluminum sheets.

Each sheet was twenty-nine and a half inches wide by twenty-three and a half inches tall. I can still remember the trouble my brother and I had in calculating that half inch in almost every measurement we needed, as Dad wouldn't let us scrape anything. This aluminum was, of course, for the inside of the corn crib. We lined the floor with aluminum and the walls with aluminum and stopped up every hole in the gap between the top of the wall and the roof of the barn. Dad found a massive piece of tree trunk; as I remember, it was about three and a half feet high and about two feet across. Dad fixed it to the floor at the inside wall of the crib, the wall facing out into the barn. There he cut a hole in the wall and built a metal chute protruding out of the corn crib. So, when we cut corn, we could place a bucket under the shoot, and our cut corn fell right into it. Dad would buy a pickup load of field corn from the farmers around our county. Field corn was the hard corn used in making animal feed. Randy and I would have to open the small door on the outside wall and shovel all the corn from the bed of the truck into the corn crib. Seal the small opening back up tight. We thought we had a dry, rat-free, safe place to store our corn for the winter. Turns out it was dry and safe, but I'm not sure anything we had could keep the rats out. After some months and deep into winter, Dad had had enough of the rats.

The droppings, the gnawed holes right through the aluminum, and, worst of all were the empty corn cobs left after the rats had eaten all the corn. We knew they had made their nests in and under the big pile of corn in the crib. We told Dad we would move the corn pile from one side of the crib to the other, and when the rats ran out, we would kill them. Dad agreed, and away we went. Now, when I say we, I mean my brother Randy, my cousin Mark, and my best friend John. The four of us went into the crypt armed with shovels, pitchforks, and some big sticks. We left the crib door open so it felt more open and the dust could get out. Then we started moving the corn. It didn't take long for the first rat to make a run for it. It blasted out of the corner and around the base of the wall and somehow managed to get past all of us and out through the open door. So now, we knew we had to close the door to finish off the rest of the rats. We closed and tied the door shut, then began moving the corn again. In no time at all there was another rat running frantically around the crib until someone struck a blow that counted, and the rat was dead. As we moved more corn, there were more rats, and we got pretty good and quick at killing them. Once we had moved the entire pile of corn to the other side, we had had enough and stopped to count the rats. I don't remember how many we got, but it was significant, and we decided that every few months we would do it again, although looking back I believe it was fun for us more than protecting the corn.

The nastiest structure on the farm, in my opinion, was the chicken house. Chickens poop all the time and anywhere; it doesn't matter where they are. The smell alone on a cold winter day would take your breath away. In the summertime, the ammonia from their urine made the smell very unpleasant, and the chicken house was not a place to be. The way you feed chickens is you spread their feed across the ground so they can scratch and peck for it. It's their natural way of eating. Their feed, most of the time, included coarsely ground field corn, which the rats just loved. Now, in the chicken house, the rats would dig tunnels. They had tunnels all under the ground, and many times, you would sink into one of the tunnels they had dug too close to the surface, all the way up to your ankle. One day, Dad found a dead chicken that had been killed by the rats. He could tell it was the rats, as the chicken's throat was the only thing damaged; that's where they lapped the blood. Dad announced that we were going to flood them out. Randy and I had no idea what that meant, but we were sure it was going to be fun.

On the day of the flooding, I had asked Mark and Bones to come over, and help, and my older brother J.D. came and my cousin Larry. Now, J.D. and Larry were a lot older than us by some ten years, so they were kind of in charge. Early that morning Dad had told Randy and me to gather all the small pieces of wood we could find, bricks, broken concrete blocks, anything that could be used to stop up a rat hole. We had done as he said and piled them all up beside the chicken house. Dad had connected enough hose to reach the chicken house from the house, and it was lying there, ready to go. Mark and Bones came riding up on their bikes, and I and Randy were showing them all we knew about the process. We were going to stop up most holes and only leave open the ones we can watch. Randy and I had already asked Dad if we could use our four ten shotguns to shoot the rats. I guess he figured four-armed boys frantically shooting rats as they ran for their lives would not be a good thing, so we had to get our walking sticks or a pitchfork. Finally, my older brother and Larry showed up, and we could begin. Dad turned the whole process over to J.D., and he began telling us which holes to stop up. After several minutes of stomping things into the open holes, we felt like we had them cornered, and Larry turned the water on.

The hose had been stuck as far down a hole as it could go. Now, all we had to do was wait and kill the rats as they ran out of the hole. We all stood there, our eyes fixed on the hole we were given to watch, waiting. It seemed to take a long time; suddenly, I heard Mark swinging his stick violently at the ground. I saw Randy stabbing the ground with his three-pronged pitchfork. Then, there he was, a rat's head that came poking out of my hole. I swung my stick as hard as I could and came right down on the mark where I had seen the rat. But the rat was already out of the hole and gone.

"You boys have got to be quicker than that!" Dad yelled as he was walking back and forth trying to watch all of us at the same time.

This was serious stuff to me and Randy, Mark, and Bones, and we stood there repeatedly swinging as those rats came running out of their holes. I don't remember us killing a single rat, but the excitement of drowning the rats out of the chicken house was intense.

The other chicken house on the farm was for the baby chickens Dad bought each spring. It was half of the old calf barn, and we had fenced it in and built some roosts and feeders. In early spring, we would build up a small pen inside the house, with lights for warmth and small feeders to get the chicks growing. Once they were big enough, we would take the incubator down and store it away for the next spring.

Dad would buy four hundred baby chickens each spring to replenish the laying hens that were too old to lay anymore. He would buy a mixed lot, meaning he would get about two hundred roosters and two hundred hens. When they got old enough to tell the roosters from the hens, we would go in and catch the hens and move them to the main chicken house. The roosters would be killed and butchered and put in the freezer for food.

Before the culling of the hens, while there were four hundred chickens in this small space, the rats would move in and thrive on the feed that was put down. We only did this a couple of times, and it was really for fun more than anything else, although we were taking care of a rodent problem too.

We waited till it was eleven o'clock or so at night, then Randy and I were joined by my friends John and Mark. We taped flashlights to our pellet guns and crawled into the chicken house. We sat in a way so that we were not straight across from one another, and we made sure we knew where each person was sitting. Then, we turned off our flashlights and waited in the dark. We waited until we could hear the rats scurrying around in the loose straw. Someone would count to three in a loud whisper; on three, the excitement started. We flipped on our flashlights, and the rat that happened to be right in front of us got shot. Now, we killed several rats this way because after the shot, we would reload and repump our pellet guns, turn off our lights, and the wait started again. Here is the interesting thing, though: when the lights came on, the rats in the light froze, giving you a chance to take the shot. However, all the other rats ran for cover. This meant that the rats would run over our legs and all over the place. John quit doing this after a rat ran up his pants leg, causing him to jump up and dance around till the thing fell out.

Growing up on a farm back in the sixties was never boring as long as there were rats to chase.

Bikes/Running the Roads

I don't remember when I built my first bike as it was something we just did; I was probably ten or eleven years old. It didn't seem like anything out of the ordinary. Looking back on it now, though, I can see that for many kids, the thought of building your own bicycle was, well, something out of the ordinary. My uncles had piled a bunch of old bike bodies, parts, and tires up in the woodshed behind Mamaw's house we had no idea where they came from, and we were allowed to use them as we saw fit. That's where my current bike had come from; we had pieced it together from the parts there. It was a rough ride, and I couldn't keep up with the store-bought ones my cousins had. The chain would fall off randomly, and I would have to stop and flip the bike over and put the chain back on. Not a big deal, but the others would scarcely wait for me, so I had to catch up.

All through my childhood, I was only given one new bicycle, a purple Western Flyer. I was so proud of that bicycle. I washed it and kept it in the pump house so the dew wouldn't fall on it. Oiled the chain and pedals with old motor oil before each ride. Never leaned it up against anything so it wouldn't get scratched. Well, that lasted about a week; then my cousin Mark and I banana the seat, which was to loosen the bolts and beat the seat with a bat until it had a nice U-shape that fit my butt just right. Tighten everything back up and now I had a real street-worthy bike. Now, my old bicycle would go to my little brother, who was riding a different bike we had built; it was even worse than mine.

Having a bike meant freedom. I could ride it down to my Mamaw's house, where Mark lived with his mom and two sisters in a trailer, but that was as far as I was allowed to go, and if we got caught beyond there, it would certainly mean Dad's belt. That was fine, though, because it was about a quarter mile on the blacktop, which meant speed and racing and jumping—the possibilities were endless. We were always coming up with new things to do on our bikes. We rode back and forth on that quarter of a mile of blacktop from Mamaw's house to the top of our lane so many times, usually just because we could. We were the kings of that little stretch of blacktop road, weaving our bikes back and forth from side to side as we went back and forth from our house to Mark's house, only occasionally having to move for a car. We built a small bridge over the ditch and cut a path into the woods so we could be riding down the road and then just disappear into the woods without stopping. We worked on that little project for days, making a clean, quick break from the road into the woods so we could hide if we needed to. As with many projects, though, once the luster and excitement wore off, we abandoned it for something new.

One day, my mom asked us if we could ride all the way around to Frazier's store and get her a couple of things. My brother and I couldn't believe what we were hearing all the way to Frazier's store. That seemed like a long way; that seemed like a big, exciting new level of our bike riding. We gladly accepted our mom's order and set about putting a basket on the front of my bike to carry her groceries. In just a few minutes we had fixed a small woven basket to the handlebars and were ready to undertake our new mission.

"It should only take you boys about an hour to get there and get back. Don't go anywhere else, and don't stop along the way. Straight there and straight back." Mom told us very sternly. We knew that if we broke her rules, we wouldn't be allowed to do this again and probably get a whipping as well.

We were so excited we could barely ride our bikes. As we headed off on this amazing adventure, I began to wonder about it. Would we be able to ride that far? What about the big hill leading up to the store? None of this doubt slowed me down or even caused a moment of hesitation.

As we approached Mamaw's house, which was our old boundary, and went past it around the curve and down into the straightaway through Cannonsburg, I suddenly realized that now we would be able to ride to the store when we wanted; our boundaries had just changed. As we rode through the straightaway on Cannonsburg Road, both sides of the road lined with houses, I felt like I was the king of the road. The small neighborhood seemed different from the seat of my Western Flyer; it felt as if it was now my own backyard. Even more so, like I had conquered a new land, and it was mine to ride through any time I wanted, and no one could stop me. We rode on past the houses, and as we crossed the small bridge that ran over Marsh Run. It was there; I had another realization. This meant that we could maybe ride our bikes here and fish in the bigger part of the creek. My mind was racing as we rounded the big curve and headed down the pretty straight section of the road toward the four-way stop. As we approached the last house before the intersection, I could clearly hear two dogs barking. When we were in front of the house, the two dogs came rushing out of their yard straight at us, barking and growling like they wanted to rip our legs off. Standing up on our bikes, I heard my little brother shout a cussword followed by Go! We pedaled as hard and fast as we could and outran those dogs. Though looking back on it now, I'm not sure we were ever in any real danger.

When we came to the four-way stop at the bottom of the big hill going up to the store, we just kept on riding, trying to keep our speed up as much as possible. As we climbed the hill, I was doing fine on my new store-bought bike, but my little brother had already given up and was pushing his old spare parts bike. I stopped and waited for him to catch up. We walked the rest of the way to the top of the hill and then coasted down the little grade to the store. We pulled up in front of the store and laid our bikes down. I took a moment to look around and let the fact that we were all the way around here in Cannonsburg, on our own, without Mom or Dad looking over our shoulders. I could see the top of the elementary school from here. We are really at the store with no mom or dad to keep us in line. What a day, I thought as I went into the store.

Joy Frazier, one of my mom's close friends and the owner of the store, was there and asked what she could do for us. We proudly told her what Mom wanted, and she helped us get it. We paid for it with the money Mom had given us, and Joy asked if we wanted a piece or two of candy. We were quick with both our yeses and what we wanted.

With the groceries in the basket on my bike, we headed back home. We had to push our bikes up the small hill that ran in front of their little store, but once we were at the top, man, we coasted all the way down to the four-way stop and made the turn without even pedaling once. After we rounded the intersection and started pedaling, we both suddenly remembered the dogs at the two-dog house. Which it became known as from that day on. We stood up and pedaled hard and were flying as we sailed past their house. This time, though, there were no dogs, not even a bark. My brother and I giggled as we rode past that house and continued home.

As we topped the gravel lane that headed down to our house, I stopped and took a moment to let the event of the day, of my life so far, sink in.

As we grew and rode bikes more and more and further and further, it seemed as though we were always on a new adventure, finding a new fishing spot or previously unknown apple or cherry tree we could swipe fruit from.

Then, one summer, my cousin Mark got a ten-speed bike. Oh, what a beautiful piece of machinery this was. Only he was allowed to even touch it, let alone ride it. That thing was amazing; he could linger behind us and then shift gears and pass us like we were sitting still. Of course, all we wanted to do was ride the new bike, and we pleaded with Mark to let us just have one ride. He would laugh and, with an evil little grin, just shake his head or mouth the word no. But one day, we were riding around to Frazier's store for something, and when we came to the curve before the straightaway leading to the four-way stop, Mark asked if I wanted to ride the ten-speed. I was so honored that he would let me ride it I could barely muster the breath to say yes. We stopped, and as we switched bikes, he gave me the rules. I couldn't go above fifth gear. I had to stop at the four-way stop and wait for the rest, and he didn't want me to go too fast. I eagerly agreed to all his rules; I probably would have paid him if I needed to. I hopped on and took off. It was higher than my bike, and I didn't like the handlebars. They were the typical bent-down-under, so I had to lean way down to hold them. I was riding along feeling great, taking my time, when Mark rode up beside me and asked if I wanted to shift to tenth gear. All I could do was nod, and he reached over as we were riding side by side and shifted the bike into its biggest gear. Before I knew it, I was going faster than I'd ever gone on a bike, and with only a little bit of the ride left till I reached the four-way stop, I was going to go as fast as I could. The only thing between me and the four-way stop now was the two-dog house. For a fleeting moment, I heard the faint barking of a dog; then I realized, to my horror, that one of the dogs had left the yard and was running as fast as it could toward me. The dog ended up straight in front of me, and I hit it. As the dog left its feet and was turned onto its side, its body stopped my bike's momentum almost instantly, and I found myself flying over the handlebars. I was horizontal, flying through the air for what seemed like forever. I came down onto the edge pavement where all the gravel and debris had collected. I landed on the palms of my hands first, followed by my chin, then my chest, and finally my knees, as I scraped and tumbled down the road.

Once I stopped and checked that I was still breathing, I looked down at my bloody hands and chest. I looked back, and Mark and everyone were looking at the bike. I stood up and walked back to where the bike had stopped. Fortunately, the only damage to the bike was the tape on the handlebars that had been scraped off in a couple of places. That was enough, though, for Mark not to speak to me for several days. He just jumped on his ten-speed bike and headed home, probably crying, but I can't say for sure. The dog was standing in the yard, still barking and running around, so I knew he'd be ok. I bled all the way home, and it took weeks for the road rash to heal. But it did heal, and Mark did speak to me again and let me ride his bike too. Looking back, we were so free in those days, with or without our bikes. The only decision we had to make was which direction to go and what to do when we got there.

Matchbox City

Rural eastern Kentucky in the late nineteen sixties and early nineteen seventies. The air was clean; the work was hard; the food was fried or smothered in gravy. We had three channels on our black and white TV, and if our father was watching, we had no choice but to watch what he was watching. During the day, when there was no work to be done and we could play, there wasn't much to choose from. Throwing a baseball, playing marbles, or some other made-up game was about all we had to choose from, that is, until we discovered Matchbox City.

Just outside of our yard fence was a creek that ran through the cow pasture on our property. Across that creek was a small patch of flat pastureland just before the hill started up very steeply into the sloped upper pasture. After the upper pasture came our property fence line, then across the blacktop road and into the woods up to the top of the ridge. However, cutting through the hill on our property was a gully washed out by years of run-off from the culvert that crossed under the blacktop road. We treated the gully like a waste area on the property. There wasn't enough water to make a creek for fishing or damming it up, in fact, if it didn't rain for a while, there was no water in it at all. One day, we realized this gully exposed the soft, pliable red clay so common in Kentucky. We found that it served our needs very well for building roads and stick houses, bridges, and anything our minds could dream up. My brother and I discovered Matchbox City by accident one day while exploring the gully. We simply dug out places to sit and, in our minds, hide from whoever might want to chase us. While sitting there in the shade of the high wall of the gully we realized the clay could be manipulated and flattened into roads or who knew what. We quickly squared off our lots and declared our boundary lines. Little did we know how long we would play in Matchbox City or how many lessons would be learned there.

Matchbox cars were a common Christmas gift and stocking stuffer, so my brother and I had several between us. We had always shared them, swapping back and forth. They never really meant much until now. Now there was Matchbox City and suddenly, my matchbox cars were very important to me. So, after some friendly horse trading, light arguing, pushing, and shoving, we got the cars divided. Next was the official layout of property lines in the gully. This too, required good negotiation skills, my brother and I arguing with one another and even the occasional pulling up his little fence line and throwing it as far as I could. Only to turn back and see my little brother had not only put down a new fence, but I had lost land in the fray. But, after an afternoon of tense land grabbing, we had it figured out.

Next came the tools. Now we knew we couldn't bring any of Dad's good tools over to play in the dirt; that would never be allowed. So, we went to the tool shed.

The tool shed was a small room built onto the end of the barn. It was a mecca of old rusting tools, parts, nuts, bolts, and nails. Some of the items we knew what they were like telephone pole cross supports. A long, narrow strip of metal with a three-quarter inch hole drilled in each end. Dad had a whole big stack of these things, but I am not sure why. But there were also things we had no idea of, like random chunks of steel that looked like they had been pinched off the main piece. Buckets and buckets of old rusty nails. We knew all about those because when dad needed nails, he would send me and my brother to the tool shed to not only pick through the buckets and get just the right size nail, but we also had to straighten enough of those old rusty nails to do whatever job he needed. A very tedious job that always ended with some very sore fingers.

As we rifled through the buckets and boxes that were on the work bench, under the workbench and stacked precariously on narrow shelves along the walls, there was excitement. Each of us felt like we needed to get the best tools so the other one would be envious. It's a brotherly thing, I guess. Once we had enough makeshift tools to begin, we headed back to Matchbox City. It only took a few minutes to realize this was going to be a great way to spend days of free time.

The gully we were playing had very steep sides, with only a few places that were not as steep. The clay was hard to dig out by hand, and once removed, it was gone, so we had to be careful and think through each time we dug the clay away. We dug out places to sit and kneel on the steep sides of the gully. This clay was carefully collected and staked up so we could use it to build things later. There was a big popular tree growing from the bottom of the gully exactly where matchbox city was, which provided shade for some areas during some times of the day. Though back then I didn't recall the sun, ever being a problem.

As I remember, we started by finding the place we wanted to put our tiny make-believe houses, and we would build out from there. Finding just the right spot was a matter of surveying the small piece of land we had carved out and envisioning the entire layout. My brother and I spent several days finding better tools to work with. Cutting small sticks and pieces of small-diameter grapevine for fences. Splitting thin slats of wood from scrap boards for rooftops and walls. Hammering the clay into roads and parking lots for our tiny cars and living in our make-believe city. We had the roads dug out and level we pounded them to a smooth surface the cars would roll very nicely on. We started at the top of the gully and dug a road to the bottom of the gully, twisting back and forth like a mountain railroad. We built up turn walls, or that's what we called them, at each corner so we could let out cars go, and they would roll smoothly all the way to the bottom of the hill.

Then, our cousins found us, and of course, they wanted their piece of land, their piece of matchbox city. So, the negotiations started all over again; they went something like this. Today I'm friends with my cousin Mark so I'll gladly deed him out a nice section of the city. My brother, not wanting to be outdone, gave a nice chunk to our cousin Bones. Now, the fence lines were a constant issue again as each of us was either enemies or friends depending on the day, what was said, or who let borrow what.

We found ways to make the roads as smooth as we could using a little water and flattening tools like pieces of pipe to roll out the bumps. We had an old hoe that we used to excavate new areas. We even found a use for those telephone pole cross-member supports from the tool shed. They made great platforms for building bridges and ramps. We found that, except for a few times when we were feuding over something, we shared our land, tools, cars, and even ideas.

This went on for the entire summer. We couldn't wait for our chores to get down so we could finish the new road, tunnel, or homestead layout. Then, there were those rainy days. Rainy days were filled with angst and worry because the rain could wash away everything. The clay would seem to just melt away, leaving a jumbled mess to clean up after the rain stopped and the clay had dried enough to play in again, sometimes, it took a week before we could get back in there. There was a thin line between building and creating in Matchbox City and playing in the mud.

The lessons we learned there in that washed-out gully, as it turns out, were lifelong lessons. Lessons in building structures, repurposing of tools, finding new materials, and how to use them. We learned patience by spending hours gently tapping and rolling out a new road, making it so smooth that the cars would roll on it just like a hardwood floor. Negotiating skills, trading this tool for that car or trying to get a bigger piece of Matchbox City. At one time I owned several parts of the city, and my brother and cousins had to pay me tolls for crossing my land. Things like building materials, unlimited use of a dump truck, and chunks of clay. Whatever we could bargain with. But most of the lessons we learned were about friendship and how important each one of us was to the others; even if we never said it out loud, we all knew it, and we know it to this day.

Music

Music has always been in my life; sometimes it was my dad sitting on the porch playing his 1953 Martin guitar. Other times, I would walk up to the head of the holler, where Harlan Sparkman would be sitting in his swing under a massive beech tree, playing his banjo claw-hammer style. It always amazed me that they could make music with these instruments. Music has always fascinated me, and that fascination keeps me playing that old 1953 Martin to this day.

My mother and father traveled around to churches in eastern Kentucky, singing for the church's congregations. The church would take up collections and pay them a few dollars for this. My mother would sing old gospel hymns, and Dad would play the guitar and sing a low harmony. I was only a baby while this was going on, but my mother told me this story about that time in our lives. I was between one and two years old, and they would take me to the church where they were playing. Dad would open his guitar case and put it up against the wall in the pulpit. Mom would sit me in Dad's open guitar case and give me Dad's keys to play with. According to Mom, I would sit there quietly and play with those keys while they performed. I love that old story, and even though I can't really remember those nights and those church services, I like to imagine them and the sound of Dad playing rhythm guitar and Mom's angelic voice singing those traditional hymns.

My dad taught me how to play the guitar. I would sit and watch him play, and I so wanted to play just like him. He played strictly rhythm and was heavy on the bass strings. When he finally said he would teach me, I was so excited. He got the guitar out and sat me on the couch and explained my first lesson. I had to be able to form the three chords that make the key of G. Those chords are G chord, C chord, and D chord. So, my exercise was just catching the G chord and making one strum on all the strings. Catch the C chord and strum only the strings for that chord. Then, catch the D chord and strum those strings.

I did this for many hours, just knowing that it would be the way to learn how to play music. I finally got to the point that I could catch the chord and strum and move to the next chord and strum pretty quickly and without much thought. I was so proud to show my dad what I could do. He watched me go through those chords several times; he smiled and moved me to my next lesson. That was the rhythm part. He explained it like this: rhythm has two parts, the beat and the strum. He explained as he slowly played the rhythm. My new lesson was to hold the G chord and simply play the beat and strum until I could do it with rhythm. Then, hold the C chord and play the beat and strum, and then the D chord. This is where I jumped ahead because I learned to do that very quickly, and I knew the next thing was going to be playing the rhythm while changing the chords. I got this down quickly, also, and I was ready to learn a song. Dad showed me how to play and sing an old standard called Will the Circle Be Unbroken. I played that song and sang the chorus until I'm sure everyone in the house was sick of it. That's how I learned to play rhythm guitar and still play it today, with as much excitement as when I was a kid just learning. I went on by myself to learn as many songs as I could. Back then, all we had was a record player, so I would sit for hours picking that needle up and moving it back to listen to a chord or lick over and over until I could do it myself. Carter Stanley, Bill Monroe, and Lester Flatt were my main influences. Later on, people like Charlie Waller and John Starling were who I tried to sing and play like.

As I kept on playing and learning each day, I didn't realize I had gotten good at playing rhythm guitar until one day, I was sitting outside on the porch playing the guitar, and Dad sat down beside me. He listened to me play several old bluegrass songs. He smiled and gave me this piece of advice.

"Don't play other people's songs; write your own." I have written more than fifty songs and recorded several of them, though I do play lots of covers as well. I knew by Dad's smile he approved of how I was playing that old guitar.

Another piece of advice he gave wasn't really advice at all but a statement, and as I think about it now, it was the moment in time when, without saying it, he was giving me his old guitar. Because I don't remember him playing the guitar after that. I was playing one summer afternoon in my favorite spot. I had built a small bench under the cherry tree that grew between the garden and the hog pen. I was sitting in the shade of that tree, and Dad walked up and listened as I played a Johnny Cash song I had learned.

"Son, this old guitar will take you places you couldn't even imagine if you let it." He said this with a serious tone in his voice. Dad just smiled, turned, and walked away. I didn't really appreciate his words until much later in my life when I found myself sitting on Bill Monroe's bus in Greenup County, Kentucky, simply having a conversation with him. That old guitar has taken me to places I never would have imagined, and because of that, I will be grateful to my dad for teaching me how to play rhythm guitar.

Over the years I have played music in so many places, I can't remember them all. I've played on the largest of stages in front of a packed opry house in West Virginia. Played in a mule barn in Ohio in January. It was so cold we could barely sing, but there were people there listening, and I guess that's all it takes for a performer to have someone to listen. Sorghum festivals, city parades, grand openings, bluegrass festivals, and everything in between.

Once, we joined a bluegrass band contest at a festival in Greenup County, Kentucky. We were the only band that signed up, so instead of sending us away, they let us play a set on the stage. We played just before the headliner, Bill Monroe. After we were done, we waited around backstage, listening to Bill Monroe and his Bluegrass Boys. When they were done, and off the stage, his manager asked if we wanted to visit with the father of bluegrass music. Of course, we said yes and climbed nervously onto his bus. We sat there for twenty minutes or so, just chatting with Bill Monroe. Asking him questions he had probably heard a thousand times, and he patiently answered each one, we even got his autograph. Over the years I've been invited to play very posh parties; I've played for governors and senators. I have met several celebrities from bluegrass and country music. All because of that old guitar. Dad taught me how to play guitar, but another man taught me how to play music and perform.

Willard Miller Jr., AKA June Miller, was a fiddle player and the father to one of my best friends, a kid. John Miller and I were best friends and remain friends today. We hunted and fished together, played in the snow, and rode inner tubes down frozen tracks of ice we had made. We even worked together helping my uncle Jim build houses. But it was a day at high school, I believe during our freshman year, that John mentioned his dad played fiddle. I was intrigued, so I asked John if maybe I could get his dad to play fiddle with me. John set it up, and I was so excited to go. But as I walked in, I began to question my abilities and started getting really nervous.

June was so patient with me, and eventually he and I formed a close friendship. I would go back to John's house, and I and John would sit and play guitar with June as he played those old fiddle tunes for hours. John would lose interest and end up just sitting and watching, and eventually, he would go and do something else. But I would sit there and play as long as June would saw on that old fiddle. He told me to work on two tunes. One was something I already knew, Will the Circle Be Unbroken, and the other tune was Orange Blossom Special.

"If you can play those two songs, well then you can play anything in between," June said, smiling under his thick mustache. I played those two songs along with the records I had at home until I could play them in my sleep.

There were a lot of times I would go to John's house with my guitar to just play with June as he played fiddle tunes. John and his little brother George and my little brother would go off and do something else, but I would sit there for hours and play those old tunes with June. He would drink his Pabst Blue Ribbon beer, and I would try my hardest to play along with him.

"Listen for the changes. Can't you hear those changes?" He would say sometimes with a little frustration in his voice. One evening, when I was fifteen, we were sitting on his porch playing, and he ran out of beer.

"Think you can drive that old Cutlass?" he said with a little smile.

He had been drinking a lot, and he knew he couldn't drive, so it was with great enthusiasm that I climbed behind the wheel and headed for Kenova, West Virginia, the closest place to our dry county to buy beer. I had been driving for a few years in the hayfields and even occasionally on a short trip on the road, but this was the first time I'd be driving a long way and even through town. For me, this trip bonded me and June Miller together forever as friends, and I will never forget it or ever forget the wisdom he bestowed on me in those evenings playing fiddle tunes as the sun went down.

While I was learning to play the guitar, my little brother was learning to play the banjo; he was very good at it too. At one point our dad decided we needed to take music lessons, so he set us up with Les Thornberry, a local music store owner in Ashland. My brother and I weren't sure whether we wanted to take lessons or what to expect. When we arrived at the shop, our dad just dropped us off and said he'd be back in an hour. We walked in carrying our instruments and waited while Mr. Thornberry prepared. Now, my brother and I played bluegrass music and had gotten pretty good at playing along with the records Mom and Dad had, so we didn't think we needed lessons, but here we were. The first thing my brother pointed out was Mr. Thornberry's shoes; they were white and looked like alligator skin or something. As he sat us down at the piano with our instruments, we found those shoes to be funnier and funnier. He was trying to teach us notes and scales and how to read music, very serious stuff, but all we could see were those white shoes. We became so disruptive that Mr. Thornberry decided to split us up. He kept Randy there and sent me into a different room with a young man who was to teach me all about the guitar. This young man was showing me power bar chords and showing me ways to stretch my fingers. This was not what I signed up for; I wanted to learn bluegrass. After an hour, we put our instruments in their cases and went out the door laughing hysterically about those dang white shoes. As we climbed into the car with Dad to head home, we both announced that we weren't going back. We explained the piano and finger stretches and those white shoes. Dad was giggling along with us and agreed that we wouldn't go back, which was a relief to us, but I bet even more of a relief to Mr. Thornberry.

My cousin Bones had been learning to play the mandolin as well, and he was pretty good at it too. With all this and June's sons John and George playing as well, John played the guitar, and George played the bass. June asked my uncle Fred to join us, and suddenly, we were in a band. I was so excited to be a part of a band that I couldn't wait each week to get back to John's house to practice.

The Boyd County Bluegrassers was what we called ourselves, and I remember June being very clear with his assignments. I would be the lead singer; my little brother would sing harmony, and my uncle Fred would fill in either baritone or bass vocals. The others would sing small parts as needed. We practiced those songs over and over until we had them down. June would direct us and tell us what we needed to do and where to stand, and how to make eye contact with the audience.

Our first time playing on a stage in front of people was at the Catlettsburg Senior Citizen's Hall. I was bouncing off the walls with excitement. I had all the knowledge given to me by my dad for playing this old guitar and from June for performing. I was ready to go, just a bit nervous. We walked out onto that stage, and there was a crowd of at least twenty people. I never thought about anything except hitting my marks and remembering all the words. We sang our first song, and when it ended, I was surprised by the applause, and as we played on, the applause seemed to get even louder. I was hooked, and I still play those old songs and some new ones to this day. In bands like Cross Creek in Kentucky, the Wirebeaters in Florida, and finally, Sycamore Shade, also here in Florida. The people I've met and the places I have been because of that old guitar are some of the very best friends and memories I have, and I cherish each one to this day.

Drive-ins – Running the Roads

When I turned sixteen and got my driver's license it seemed like the whole world opened for me. I had been driving for several years already, in the hay fields and on short trips with my dad or older brother when they would let me drive. But now I was able to go as I wanted, when I wanted, and most importantly, where I wanted. Dad had horse traded a butterscotch yellow Chevy Vega from my uncle, and it was mine. I spent days just driving around the roads I had always been on. Going to my friend's house where I had always been going and running to the stores I had been to a thousand times.

The difference I guess, was that I was going to these places on my terms now. It certainly felt like freedom at the time. I ran that Vega with my cousins and friends until the transmission failed. We would run up and down Keyser Creek Road. Keyser Creek Road was a gravel road that went up a steep grade and crossed Skyline Drive. At the crossing, the gravel road had been built up to meet the surface of Skyline Drive this build-up made a ramp of sorts. My cousin Bones was driving an old Ford pickup and he and I would run up and down that road, following as close as we could without hitting each other. We would race and pass each other at speeds that, looking back, were just stupid. The dust cloud we raised in the summertime was enough to have us driving blindly, though it never really stopped us or even slowed us down. Looking back on those evenings we were extremely lucky that nothing bad ever happened.

At the time, there was a show on TV called The Dukes of Hazard. A family show about two cousins and their uncle Jessie, driving around and outrunning the police. While, we were never involved in a police chase. We drove around and did some sketchy stuff. We called ourselves the Moore's of Boyd and we rode around hooting and hollering a lot. One thing we liked to do was change drivers while driving down the connecting road from the county into the city; Route sixty was all we ever called it. Whoever was in the passenger seat would climb out the window and into the back of the truck. Cross the bed to the driver's side and climb into the driver's seat. At the same time, the driver would scoot over and only have their left foot on the gas and their left hand on the steering wheel. All this happened while we were doing about sixty-five miles an hour. Then there were the strip mines. We knew how to get around the gates if there were gates. And we would race all around the old strip-load roads. Some had four-feet or eight-feet high walls, and we would jump our cars off those at speed, thrashing us and our cars to the breaking point.

After my Vega lost its transmission and, I sold it to a friend of mine. He had to drive it home about six miles in reverse. That was quite the trip as I drove in front of him, kind of clearing the road. I bought a nineteen sixty-six Chevy long-wheelbase pickup truck; it was a tank. Made of steel from bumper to bumper. The truck was hand-painted with a light blue body and a white cab, with a brown topper mounted on the bed. This also meant that I could go to the drive-in theatre when I wanted. The Trail Drive-in theatre was the local drive-in, and it was one of the only things to do there in the Asland area. I spent so many weekends there with my friends in the summer months. We would go to the drive-in almost every Friday and Saturday night and be there till the wee hours of the morning. I remember seeing Moonraker, the James Bond movie, fourteen weeks in a row, that's twenty-eight times I watched it, other movies ran for several weeks, and we would go anyway, as it wasn't about the movie. Lots of things happened there at the Trail Drive-in, everything from sneaking our friends in to getting alcohol, smoking pot, and of course, sex. Now I had a truck with a topper on it, so naturally, we threw an old mattress in the back and my old truck became a popular place on the weekends at the drive-in. The Trail Drive-in in the back of that old truck was the place I lost my virginity, the same was true for several of my friends.

There were other drive-ins in the area and as time went on, we found ourselves at these theatres many weekends.

One of those weekend nights began at my best friend John Miller's house. We were going to the Corral Drive-in in Flatwoods, Kentucky to see three scary movies. The first movie was called The Brood, a new horror film. The other two titles escape me now as the Brood scared the living bejesus out of me. We watched part of the second movie, something about some witches, but we didn't stay to watch all of it.

It was well after midnight by the time we got back to John's house where my truck was parked. My truck's gas gauge didn't work, so I was always guessing about how much fuel I had. On this night I had guessed wrong and ran out of gas a hundred feet of so from John's house. Embarrassed, I didn't want to go knocking on John's front door and wake everyone up, so I headed out walking home. The walk was only about three miles, I had walked it hundreds of times before, but this night was different, and I had some scary movie plot running through my head.

The night was dark with no moon, and in rural Kentucky, there were no streetlights, so only the occasional porch light helped to light my way down the road. I followed the lane John lived on and out to Marsh Hill Drive where I turned left and looked down a dark ridge road lined with trees. As I walked, I was thinking of anything I could come up with to keep that movie out of my head. The night air was still and felt wet with heavy dew, as I came to the end of Marsh Hill

Drive and started down Cannonsburg Road toward my house. From here on, the road was downhill and very curvy, it was lined with very large trees, which in many places created a canopy over the road, making the dark night even darker. There were places along this road where I couldn't see my hand in front of my face. On the right side of the road was a steep bank leading up to the woods with heavy underbrush, briars, and large trees. On the left side of the road was a fence and a steep drop-off going down into old man Jackson's cow pasture, though he rarely put his cows on this side of his property. As I walked, I would hear the occasional rustling in the leaves, and I would remember what my dad taught me about hearing sounds. He told me that I needed to identify the sound as quickly as possible, so my imagination wouldn't take over and I would get scared. So, when I heard a rustle in the leaves, I would quickly tell myself, that's an opossum or some other small animal of the night.

About three-quarters of the way home, in a particularly dark part of the walk, suddenly, there was a sound I couldn't identify quickly enough. It was the sound of air being pushed out of something at a high rate of speed. It stopped me in my tracks, and I felt a knot coming up in my stomach. There it was again, a kind of blowing noise or was it a cough or a growl? I reached into my pocket and took out my small pocketknife, I opened it and prepared for the worst. The sound came again this time, I could tell it was coming from beyond the fence, down the steep drop-off, out of old man Jackson's field. I was still frozen in my place, but I knew I had to walk on to get home, or step over and see what was making this noise. The noise continued as I stood there for what seemed like an eternity, trying to get my legs to move. Finally, I made myself step toward that side of the road; I couldn't put anything in my head to identify this sound. I slowly stepped toward the fence and looked down into the pasture. Just as my eyes made contact with the silhouette, I could barely make out in this light the noise came again, this time louder and clearer. It was a stupid cow. Old man Jackson had put his cows on this side, and they were standing just at the bottom of the steep bluff. One was blowing air through its nose, probably as a warning to me not to come down there. I smiled and put my knife away and continued to walk home. I decided not to tell anyone about this encounter with the cows and didn't for many years.

Church Nights

Growing up in rural Kentucky, my mother was deeply religious. This meant my little brother and I were held to certain standards by our mother. We were held to even higher standards by our father. Not only was he religious, but in his eyes, embarrassing or insulting our mother, even in an accidental way, was one of the worst things we could do. So, we paid attention to what we said, how we said it, and even where we said it. This was all brought to a high point at church.

We attended Rockdale Freewill Baptist Church, a small white structure located in, of course, the small community of Rockdale, which sat along Shopes Creek Road. The church had a main building with a pulpit, choir pews, and hard oak benches for the congregation to sit on. Oh, how many hours I sat and fidgeted on those hard pews. Underneath the church was the basement, a place where Sunday school classes were held and youth Bible study would take place. The basement was partitioned into four rooms with folding chairs and one long table in each room. The basement always smelled of wet paint, as the concrete blocks from which it was made would hold moisture, so the joint of the paint and block never really cured, thus producing the wet paint smell.

Church started at seven pm on Wednesdays, and everyone would be in their seats. While never assigned, there were certain seats that were reserved for certain people. The front row was for the pastor, deacons, and preachers from other churches in attendance. The second row was for the elders of the church, the folks that were there as long as I could remember being there and were there long after I stopped attending. The row next to the back row was where my mother and the other mothers sat. We had to sit in front of our mothers so we could be watched. The other seats were free for the taking, although some folks always sat in the same seat each night. The pastor, who was my uncle Arthur, would call the service to order with a call to bow our heads and pray. When he said this, every head in the building would bow. Then, the choir would slowly make their way to the choir pews, and Mrs. Stapleton would take her seat at the piano. The hymns were sung with reverence and heartfelt sincerity. After the songs, the choir would return to their seats, and the service leader would ask everyone to pray again. After that prayer, several of the congregation would stand and walk up front, where they would stand in a semi-circle and, one by one, ask the church for prayers for a sick loved one, or a family struggling with life, or just to put a blessing on someone they thought needed it. Everyone would then return to their seat, and the service leader would share a lesson he had come up with from the scriptures. Then, he would either start preaching the sermon or bring up the preacher who was going to preach the sermon. Some of these preachers were long-winded, some were loud, and some shouted with a fierceness that would put the fear of God in you if you were paying attention. We knew each one's style, so we knew how long it would be before we got out and headed home. After the sermon, the service leader would ask if there was anyone with anything on their heart that they wanted to pray about. As this was happening, some of the choir would return to their pews and begin singing softly one of many old hymns. The service leader would then open the invitation and ask for anyone without God to come down and, on bended knee, accept God into their hearts. On the nights that someone went down, and there were many, most of the congregation would follow them and kneel with them to pray. The night I was saved, the church had been released, but for some reason I felt like I wanted to stay and that I wanted to give my heart to our Lord and Savior. My uncle Fred noticed me sitting with my head down crying. He came over and grabbed me up by the arm, and led me to the altar. The other members of the church saw this, and they all came back to pray with me. I don't believe I have ever felt so safe as I did on that night. This praying could go on for some time and seemed to add hours to the service some nights. The service leader would then ask everyone to pray one more time then, with a hearty May God bless you, he would release us to go home.

My mother wanted to go to every service, and there were times when neither my father, my brother, nor I really wanted to attend, but Dad would always make either me or my brother go with her, and if we argued, he would make both of us go.

There were services on Sunday morning, Sunday night, and Wednesday night. Our mother wanted to attend all of them and would most weeks, which meant I or my brother attended all of them.

Now, as boys, we would find ways to entertain ourselves there at the church. There were several of us young boys there, and there was never a fight or any type of argument among us. Probably because we all knew what would happen if we did, we would find an empty pew and sit several feet apart, take a folded piece of paper, and play kick football. A game where you try and kick the football using your fingers through your friend's finger goalposts. It was all well and good as long as no one saw the paper football, so we had to keep it low and under the back of the pew. Another good way to pass the time was hangman; we filled untold numbers of tablets drawing and playing that game. Again, we had to keep it below a whisper, and there could be very little fidgeting and moving. In the summertime, we would, one at a time, let our mom know we had to go to the bathroom. The bathroom was outside and all the way down by the creek; it was an outhouse. One side for men and one side for women. Once we got outside, there was very little effort by our parents to get us back inside. I guess they figured at least out there they can't interrupt the service. Sometimes, our moms would stare at us and shake their heads no, making us sit there and understand who was in charge.

The church property ran down toward the creek, where there was a small flat bottom that was perfect for racing or a game of football. Just beyond the bottom was a man-made berm to keep the water from flooding up into the church during rains. Then came the creek, a small flowing stream that was never dry and always provided some type of fun. We did everything there, from building dams to channeling off streams of water for racing our homemade carved wooden boats. Catching crawdads and small minnows and keeping them in small pools we had dug. Looking for and identifying tracks of opossums, raccoons, deer, and other animals was always a discussion worth twenty or so minutes. Occasionally, we would find a ball or Frisbee that had washed downstream, and we would head back up into the little bottom to play a game of whatever ball we had found. I liked collecting the different types of river rocks; different types simply mean different colors and styles of rocks. I had no knowledge of what type of rock or stone I was looking at. I guess it was just something to do that interested me.

The most eventful thing we ever did, though, was catching water snakes. In the summertime, we would catch handfuls of these slithering reptiles, just to say we did. We always released them unharmed because there wasn't really anything you could do with a snake. When we first started catching snakes, it was simply when we found one. But then we started turning over large rocks to try and find them. One summer, we even put large pieces of plywood or other material down in the shallow, fast-running ripples to attract the snakes. We eventually built a tall rock pit on one of the sandbars, and we would catch a couple of big water snakes. We took their heads and kind of poked each one with the other one in the head, then dropped them in the rock pit. Sometimes, they would attack each other as they defended themselves. We called it snake fighting, though it was mostly snake catching, dropping, and watching them try to hide.

This all ended for me one summer evening when my cousin Keith caught a very large water snake. This thing was probably five feet long and as big as the business end of a baseball bat. It may have been the biggest snake we had ever caught. Keith was holding it and still looking for another snake to throw in the pit. When he raised up a flat piece of debris in the ripples, sure enough, there was another large water snake. Keith grabbed it with his empty hand and handed the other big snake to me. I took it by the neck just behind the head to hold it. I wasn't paying much attention to it, as most of our snakes were much smaller, and we could handle them with one hand. This snake was different, though, and began to wrap its body around my arm. Before I knew what was happening, the snake had wrapped itself completely around my arm all the way up to my elbow, and then it began squeezing. As I realized what was happening, a terror-filled my little body like I had never known. To this day, I can feel that snake squeezing down on my bony little forearm. I let out a terror-filled yell and flung that snake as far as I could in whatever direction I was standing. There was no thought of how or where to release this snake; there was only terror and get it off me. Once the snake was gone and off my arm and I came back to my senses, the rest of the boys were just looking at me. I remember trying to explain what had happened, but they only saw that the biggest snake we had ever caught was gone. Snake hunting, catching, and fighting never had much appeal to me after that harrowing evening at Rockdale Church. But the many life lessons learned there have proven invaluable. I was saved and baptized at that little church, and I remember all my friends being there being a part of something that felt bigger than any of us.

Jackpot— Finding Lake Bonita

In the hills of Kentucky, the outdoors was the place to be. Hunting, fishing, trapping, hiking, camping, and even working were almost always outdoors. My favorite thing was fishing. I just couldn't get enough of sitting along the small streams and fishing for whatever small fish or crawdads I could catch. My dad liked to fish, but it wasn't as important to him as it was to me, so the rare times that we went fishing never lasted long enough, and I always left disappointed, wanting more. Then, one summer day, I was hiking up the hill toward my Mamaw Nancy's house and came out on Terrapin Ridge. As I walked along the road with no real destination, I realized I hadn't gone into the woods past the road. So, as boys do, I took off down the hill to see what I could see. The woods were the same as every other forest in our area. Large oak, poplar, and beech trees and lots of assorted small trees and bushes. As I made my way down the hill, I was looking for anything that might be different or catch my interest. I came all the way down to the bottom of the holler still looking for something to explore. As I came out of the woods into what I thought was a pasture, I quickly realized it was a lake, a big lake, a really big lake. My heart raced as I realized just what I had happened upon. This was not like Ross's Lake; this was a big, deep lake. I couldn't believe what I had found.

My mind started planning what I could do here. I could bring over some fishing stuff and leave it here hidden. I was so excited I could barely contain myself. My mind was racing with questions like, who owned this lake? Could I get permission to fish here? Would my dad allow me to come over here to fish? Do I tell Randy, my little brother? I was thinking through all of this as I made my way up and around the lake to see how big it was. I quickly realized there were people fishing and cars parked down at the dammed-up end. What was this place? I thought as I squatted down to stay out of sight. I decided to head back home and gather up some fishing stuff to come back and at least fish here in this little cove. So, I started back up the hill toward our house.

Once I was back at our house, I had to figure out what I needed to do to get back over there and try to fish. By this time, I had a rod and reel. It was a Zebco 202 with a short rod. I went through my stash of fishing items I had collected. Some fishing lines, sinkers, and some hooks of different sizes. I put them all in a small box I had and decided I would tell my brother, and we could head back over there the next day. When I told my brother I didn't think he believed me, he was willing to go with me.

The next day, after our chores were done, we quietly headed out. We walked up the pipeline through old man Jackson's pasture, hoping his bull wasn't in there. We came out on Terrapin Ridge and walked a short distance down the road. From there we headed into the woods and down the hill to the same place I had been to the day before. My brother had brought his rod and reel too, and we made our way through the thick woods and down to the lake. There was no one fishing back in this little cove out of sight of the house at the other end. We dug some worms and began fishing. We caught some small bluegills and bass, but I wanted to move around to find what had to be better fishing spots so bad. We stayed in that little cove fishing for several hours that day, and we visited the lake several times in the next week or so.

We were at church and were talking to my cousin, who was older than me by two years, and I asked him about this mysterious lake I had found. He studied the map in his head of where I was talking about, as we were all good with directions.

"Lake Bonita," he said, "it has to be Lake Bonita." My mouth was just hanging open; he knew about this lake. I started firing off all kinds of questions about what kind of fish there are in the lake. Can anyone fish there? That's when he explained it was a pay lake. I had never heard of a pay lake. He explained that you pay a fee, and you can fish there; anyone can.

The next day, I went to my dad to ask him if he knew about Lake Bonita. He didn't know what I was talking about, but when I explained where we had found it, he studied this new information for a bit, his jawline flexing as he ground his teeth.

"Let's go check it out." He finally spoke to my excitement.

We drove over to the little road that led up to the lake. As we pulled up into the parking lot that sat on the dam, I just couldn't believe my eyes. This lake was huge, and it looked deep too. There were a couple of people fishing along the side of the lake.

"Let's go see what it costs to fish and see if they are catching anything." He said as he climbed out of the car.

Howard Crabtree was the man who owned the lake and ran the pay fishing business. Howard would later join our little church in Rockdale; this created some opportunities for fishing without paying. I was amazed that all of this was right here in walking distance from my house; I just couldn't believe it. Three dollars and fifty cents got you twenty-four hours. That was the price. We walked out of the small shop and down the path to the folks fishing. Dad asked them if they were catching anything, and they pulled up a stringer with seven or eight big catfish. I was so excited I could hardly breathe. We left, and Dad suggested we come back that weekend and try our luck.

That weekend was a huge day for me. My dad, my little brother, my uncle Arthur, and my cousins Keith, Bones, and Mark were all here and were fishing. We set our lines, and I stood there like a cat ready to pounce on the first pole that moved. That was a great day, and it went on into the night before we left. I can't recall exactly what we caught, but I'm sure we got some catfish, and I'm sure Mom fried them up for us.

Now, camping out was a normal routine for all of us; we just had to pack our limited things and let Mom and Dad know where we were going. So, when I went to Dad and asked if we could camp at Lake Bonita, he looked at me for a long time. I believe he knew what this question meant to me, and he knew I was old enough to do this as well. He made one condition: that my cousins had to go too. I was on the phone so fast calling them all to see if they wanted to go camping out and fishing at Lake Bonita. They all said yes, and their parents said yes, so we only had to wait till the day came. That day, late in the morning when our dad dropped us off at the lake and drove away, I felt like I could do anything. We quickly went and paid and set out to find the best spot to fish. We picked a spot and settled in, each of us calling certain areas as our own and making sure no one cast into our spots. That was the first night I can remember being awake all night; even though my cousins and my brother slept on the cold ground, I sat there waiting for any sign of a bite. Each one of them gave me control of their poles as they went to sleep. The next morning when they all awoke, I had tied up three large catfish and couldn't wait to get home and eat them. Our dad picked us up that morning, and I was on top of the world. When we got home, he showed us how to clean the fish and get them ready to fry. Mom put them in some water to sit, and I went to sleep. That evening for supper we had fried catfish for dinner, and my mind was on the next trip. Little did I know that evening how important Lake Bonita would be to me and how much time I would spend there.

Over that summer we camped and fished there as many weekends as possible. Mom was always willing to give me and my brother the entry fee and a couple of dollars to buy something to eat as well. Those nights of sitting around a campfire and watching your poles in the light of the fire, waiting for any movement, were special nights for me. When winter came and we were back in school, the fishing poles were put away, and we had to wait till next summer. Then we heard that in late February they were going to stock Lake Bonita with rainbow trout. My head was filled with all kinds of thoughts and dreams about catching these trout. Finally, Saturday came, and we packed up to go camp out and catch trout. The day was cold, and it was drizzling rain, but that didn't deter us. We headed up to the point, as we called it, to set up camp. We all had new and strange baits to use: canned corn and, of all things. I didn't understand the concept, but that is what we were told, so we went with it. As the evening turned into night, the cold and the rain didn't bother me, but the lack of fish biting did. I was beginning to think this was all just a cruel promotion by the owner to drum up money in the wintertime. Then, just as darkness was settling in on us, my cousin Keith got a huge bite and set the hook. When he got it in, it was, to my absolute astonishment, a rainbow trout. So, they were here, and we could catch them. My excitement carried me through a sleepless, cold, and wet night. I was the only one that stayed up all night catching these amazing trout. To be honest, though, there wasn't much sleep for anyone that night because of the cold and the rain. We spent many nights fighting in the cruel spring weather of Kentucky just to catch these fish.

Spring turned into summer, and my little brother became a regulars at Lake Bonita. We would pay our fee and head to the spot we thought was the best for the night. Typically, we liked to fish on Tuesday nights, as there weren't so many fishermen, but we did fish on the weekends too with our cousins. That's when we learned about the big fish contest. One Saturday night we were all fishing. There were several groups fishing all around the lake, and you could hear the occasional indiscernible sounds of voices carrying across the water or the splashing of someone landing a fish suddenly from across the lake.

"Jackpot!" We heard someone yell. What was that, and why did they yell it? The next morning, I went straight to Howard's little store to ask what that was about. It seems that if there are enough people paying and you pay a little extra money on Friday or Saturday night, then there becomes a pool of money called the jackpot. If you catch the biggest fish, you win the jackpot. Now the size of the jackpot depended on how many people had put in on it. But since it was a form of gambling, our mothers would never give us the money to compete. So, there were many nights we heard several yells of jackpot.

One Tuesday night my brother and I went to Lake Bonita as usual to camp and fish, but the excitement just wasn't there. Our mom dropped us off as usual, and we paid and headed to our spot. As the evening wore on and day turned into night, neither I nor my brother was really into fishing, especially sleeping on the ground. So, in the middle of the night, we decided to head home, walking. We gathered up our fishing gear, sleeping bags, and other miscellaneous items. We tied them up as neatly as we could and divided them all up. We had two choices for going home. The first was up the hill through the woods to Terrapin Ridge and then down through the woods to home. This was the shortest route, but we were carrying a lot of stuff, and it was dark. So, we decided to walk home on the road. A longer walk in miles and in time, but we knew we could do it. We headed out and walked past the little store that was attached to Howard's house and down the little lane that led up to the main road.

Once on the main road, we readjusted our loads and started walking. Neither of us wanted to go for this walk, but neither of us wanted to stay at the lake either. So, we weren't talking much, just walking and carrying our stuff. As we made our way down to the intersection and turned left up the hill toward our house, we passed several houses that were dark and still this time of night. The walk was long, and our loads were growing heavier and heavier. We pushed on through the darkness and got almost to the top of the hill. This was the last house on this side of the ridge; after it, we would be walking down the other side toward our house. As we walked silently in front of the house, we weren't focused on anything except the road and our footsteps. Suddenly, out of the darkness, it seemed to be right beside us; a large dog came barking ferociously and running toward us. My little brother let out a high-pitched shriek as I turned to face the dog, thinking I could throw all my stuff at it if it came at me. Luckily, the dog stopped at the edge of the yard and didn't really attack us, but the damage was done. We were constantly looking for dogs the rest of the way home. As we came down the hill and climbed our pasture fence, we left our stuff under a tree. We figured we could come back in the morning and collect it.

At home, we decided not to knock on the door and wake Mom and Dad up. So, we climbed into the bed of the truck with our sleeping bags. Shortly after lying down, it began to rain, so I quickly jumped into the cab of the truck and stretched out on the seat. My little brother climbed into the pump house through an unlocked window. The next morning, when Dad opened the truck door, startling me, I raised up quickly and scared him. He was going on about how we should've knocked on the door last night, but I was only interested in getting into my bed and sleeping some more. So, I slowly walked away from him and headed inside.

I fished Lake Bonita for several years, until I was out of school and working and could drive to other places to fish. However, the nights spent their camping, fishing, and growing up with the other boys are an amazing part of my childhood.

Beans, Berries, and Bees

In the summertime, along with our regular chores of feeding the hogs and chickens, milking the cows, and putting up hay, we mowed the grass in small sections each day so we could give the cut grass to the chickens. We also had to tend to what certainly felt like a never-ending garden. Our garden was the length and width of a football field, and in the hot summer months, working that much garden was a real test of our stamina and Dad's patience. Dad would start in early spring by planting lettuce and onions in a homemade covered planting bed. We had also built a large teepee and wrapped it in sheets of clear plastic, and we started our tomato plants from seeds in there. Mr McGuire would bring his tractor over and plow the garden for Dad, probably for gas money, though I never saw any money change hands. My brother and I would walk behind the plow and pick up rocks, pieces of wood, or anything that wasn't supposed to be in the garden; we piled it up on the edge of the garden to get rid of it later. Sometimes, we would grab the plow frame and lay down so the tractor would drag us along in the freshly plowed furrow. Mr. McGuire only had so much patience for that kind of nonsense and would stop the tractor and yell at us. After plowing, he would come back and run the disc harrow to break up the ground so we could plant it. Once he was done, Dad would set out the plowing furrows with a hand plow. Slowly, he would make the furrows for the potatoes first, then the corn and beans; finally, he would work in all the other vegetables. We would spend the next several days planting the garden.

We had to cut the potatoes into quarters with as many eyes on them as possible. Then, one of us had to drop two quarters in the furrow about every eighteen inches. Dad usually would cover the quarters up, because we couldn't plow deep enough with that old hand plow to cover the potatoes. Next were the beans and corn. Every twelve inches or so I would drop two kernels of seed corn, followed by my little brother dropping three half-runner green bean seeds in with the seed corn. The corn had a pink powder on it, and my hands and fingers would turn bright pink from it. Probably should've worn gloves, but who knew back then? Dad would follow us with the plow, lightly covering the seeds. The tomatoes were the hardest because we were planting young plants and not just dropping seeds. It went something like this. I would have a small bucket with twenty or so small tomato plants in the bucket sitting in some water. I had a sharp stick that I would punch into the ground about every fifteen inches or so. Drop a tomato sprout in and move to the next hole. Randy would come behind me and gently fill in the holes with dirt and pour one cup of water onto the plant; the cup was made from an old pop can. This was slow and backbreaking work, but we managed to get it done every spring. Sometimes, Dad would plant the rest of the garden by himself with sweet potatoes, peas, carrots, cabbage, and pumpkins for the hogs. Dad would let us plant some watermelon seeds around the edge of the garden as long as they didn't interfere with the rear garden. While the vegetables were growing, we would spend hours with a garden hoe and small pitchfork chopping and digging weeds out. Dad taught me how to use the hand plow in the middle of the furrow aisles, but that was a hard way to do it, and my arms would burn from the stress on my muscles. When the vegetables grew to maturity and started producing, we, of course, had to start picking them. Now, Dad thought it was better to get the vegetables picked before the dew rose in the morning and the sun got hot, and maybe it was. But I'm here to tell you that wet green bean leaves are like sandpaper when they cling to your arms, and wet corn stalk leaves can wrap around your arms and give tiny cuts, like paper cuts. Tomato vines will leave a smell on your hands that is hard to get off. Sweet potato vines will tangle around your feet, and you'll be on the ground in no time. Not to mention just the wetness of all those leaves and their dew drops. Many mornings, I came out with wet shoes and jeans. There were fun things to do too, though. Like cutting pumpkin stems and making a small slit at one end. When you blow on it, it makes a low humming noise. The gooseberry bushes that grew next to the garden always produced loads of gooseberries, and while they were still green and extremely sour, we would dare each other to put as many in our mouths as we could chew. I don't remember the record, but I'm sure my little brother holds it. We would pick vegetables all summer for dinner. We picked beans and corn by the bushel so Mom could freeze it or can it. As the summer ended, we would dig all the potatoes and sweet potatoes and store them in bins in the pump house. Tomatoes were simmered and then canned for the winter. Some tomatoes were split, and the seeds were removed and dried; these were for planting next spring. Leftover vegetables and the pumpkins were cut up into small pieces and dumped into the goulash kettle with water. We would have to keep the fire going under it for what seemed like days till the vegetables were soft. Then we fed it to the hogs. Nothing went to waste.

As spring turned into summer and the garden was coming in nicely, we would turn our attention to raspberry and blackberry picking. Raspberries were first, as they ripened before the blackberries. Mom wanted all the raspberries we could pick. She would make thickened raspberries to put over hot buttered biscuits that were so good, she would freeze the rest. Once blackberries came in, we would have blackberry cobbler, pies, and blackberry dumplings. We would rotate our patches and pick the berries once or twice a week, depending on how much rain we got. On berry-picking days, we would do up the feeding and milking, eat breakfast, and grab a water jug. The goal was to be done and back home before the dew rose and it got really hot. We knew of several big patches of wild berries, and Dad would drive us to those places and help us pick. We each had a one-gallon metal paint can that had been washed out and cleaned up. That bucket was hung from our belt buckle in the front. Now, we could use both hands to pick blackberries. We also carried an old seven-gallon lard can with its lid that Dad had cleaned up. So, all told, between our three cans and the lard can, that was ten gallons of blackberries we could get. Picking blackberries is hard, painful work. You must hike to the berry patch sometimes; that was over a mile through the woods, up over ridges, and around and up hollers. Then, you must work your way into the patch. Each vine is covered in thorns, and each patch is a twisted mess of thorny vines. We were always on the lookout for snakes, hornets' nests, yellow jacket nests, and spiders. We would use our legs to tramp down the vines so we could move through the patch, picking as we went. We could work on a patch quickly and move on to the next one. Dad always taught us to be as quiet in the woods as possible, so there was very little talking, just whispering as we emptied our small buckets into the lard can. If we needed to communicate or find one another, we whistled like a lost bobwhite quail. The others would respond with a bobwhite quail's typical call. We followed that rule, and I still practice those calls today when I'm hiking.

Now we picked a lot of berries, ten gallons at a time, and once Mom had all she needed for freezing and making jelly or jam, Randy and I could sell all we picked. That's when we really turned on the picking. My brother and I would sell those berries for one dollar and thirty-five cents a gallon, and Dad knew several folks in Catlettsburg and Ashland who were willing to buy them. Today you can buy blackberries year-round with no more work than a quick trip to the grocery store. However, they just don't taste as sweet as the ones we bled and sweated for.

Dad and his brother, Uncle Jim, kept eight or ten beehives down on Mamaw Moore's hill on the edge of the plum tree patch. Though those plum trees never really produced much in the way of plums, the blossoms were why the bees were there. At the end of summer, Dad and Uncle Jim would go down and rob the bees. A lot of the family would come around on that day to help with the honey and, of course, get some of it. I was allergic to bees, so I could never go with Dad to this job. I stayed behind with my cousins and helped the others carry the tubs of raw honey and honeycomb and pick bees out of it. One summer, I decided I was going to go help, so Dad put the big rubber gloves on my hands and taped them to my shirt sleeves. A big homemade bee mask, made from cotton fabric and screen wire, tucked way down into my shirt collar. A pair of coveralls way too big for me rounded out the ensemble. As we smoked the bees and Dad pulled the racks of honey out, I put them in the tubs for the other boys to carry down the hill to the women. I felt like I was really helping, really a part of what Dad and Uncle Jim were doing. Then, I felt a bee inside my coveralls. I ran to my dad and told him what was happening.

"Walk to the bottom of the hill slowly and take your bee stuff off real slow," he said, never really stopping what he was doing.

That was one of the longest walks I can remember. I could feel the bee inside my coveralls, and I didn't want it to sting me, so I was moving very slowly. Once down, I told my cousin Mark what was happening, and he started helping me get out of this suit. The bee mask came off first. Then he untaped the sleeves of the gloves. I felt the bee go down my arm on the inside of my shirt and into my glove. I could feel it buzzing around in there. I just knew any second it was going to sting me, and I would swell up like a balloon.

"We have to jerk the glove off quickly." Mark said, smiling. Mark took the ends of the fingers on my glove and began to count.

"One, two," Mark was smiling as he counted down. At that moment he yanked the glove as hard and fast as he could. The bee stung me as it was crushed in the wristband of the glove. It must've not gotten me good because I didn't swell or feel sick. I've outgrown my allergy to bees and have been stung many times over the years.

Mom and the other ladies would end up with dozens of mason jars full of wonderful golden honey. In the wintertime, on sunny but cold days, I, my brother, and my cousins would sneak down to open a hive. We would have an empty rack waiting so we could pull the top, take out a rack, and replace it with a new one. We had to be quick, or the bees could die from the cold. We would scrape every ounce of honey off the rack, and it tasted so good, probably because we stole it. I don't think Dad or Uncle Jim ever knew we did this; they would've been upset if they had.

We could always tell what season it was and what season was coming by what was happening on our little farm. Everything we did seemed to be in preparation for the winter months and the cold they would bring. Every year, as soon as the ground thawed and the calendar rolled into spring, we were right back at it.

The Fight

As I have said before, growing up in eastern Kentucky meant hunting, fishing, and spending lots of time outdoors. It also meant that there were traditions and rules, and everything depended on your parents' decision of when you were ready for the next phase.

My little brother and I hunted for squirrels, rabbits, quail, and grouse with our four-tens or a twenty-two rifle our father had. But the next phase, the one I was waiting for, was when I would be able to use Dad's gun. Ole meat in the pot was what Dad called it. I saw him once raise our bedroom window and shoot into a covey of quail that had settled on the creek bank across the lane in the snow. He killed ten or twelve of those things with one shot, and that was one of the best things I had ever tasted after Mom fried them just like chicken.

Squirrel season was getting close; it usually came in around the end of August, and we couldn't wait to go back into the woods hunting. In the days leading up to the opening day, we would make all our preparations. Clean and oil our guns. Count our shotgun shells. If we had saved enough allowance, we could go with Dad and buy a new box of 25 shells at Heck's department store or Western Auto.

"Don't shoot unless you're sure you will get him." Dad would always tell us.

We took wire clothes hangers, cut them, and made a squirrel pin, from which we would hang the dead squirrels by their feet from our belt. The squirrel pin was made in the shape of a baby's diaper pin, and we would use Dad's bench grinder to sharpen the end. We worked on those pins till they were as sharp as we could get them. Then there was the planning. Some seasons we went to our cousin's house, and some seasons, they stayed with us. But we would all call out directions in which we were heading that first morning. Some opening mornings were cool with heavy dew, light fog, and no wind. These were the best mornings to hunt squirrels. That first morning there were shotguns being fired all around the hollers and ridges as everyone seemed to be out hunting squirrels.

From the time I was thirteen, every squirrel season which was the first hunting season of the year to come. I would ask Dad if I could use his gun to hunt squirrels with. It wasn't that my gun wouldn't do the job or that my .410 was slowing me down; I just wanted to move to that next phase. After I turned fourteen, that next squirrel season, I was asking again.

"Not this year," Dad said, once again putting me off. I don't know if it was my sadness that again, I would have to hunt with what we all considered a kid's gun, or if he was going to do this all along. But late one morning after squirrel season started, he came and got me, and he had old meat in the pot tucked up under his arm. We walked out into the garden, which was by now basically an empty field. He had me take an old milk jug out twenty yards or so and set it down. When I got back to him, he handed me the gun. I noticed it was heavier than my four-ten and longer too.

"Show me how to load it," he said with a stern face. I knew if I blew this, it would be at least a year more before I would get another chance. I turned so the gun was pointed downrange and slid my thumb and the lever to the right, allowing the gun to break down to be loaded. Dad took out one shell and handed it to me.

"Go ahead, load it and shoot," he said now with a small smile. I shoved the shell into the gun and snapped the barrel back in place. My thumb was barely strong enough to pull the hammer back, cocking the gun. I put the twelve-gauge up firmly against my shoulder and fired at the jug. To my amazement I hit the jug, then I registered the pain in my shoulder. The gun had quite a recoil, and there was nothing but wood stock and my shoulder to catch it. I looked up at my dad and smiled as big as I could, never showing any pain or discomfort from shooting his gun. He walked away back toward the house, and I ran to catch up with him. He just smiled and nodded, letting me know I could use his gun this season. Later that very day, I was going to go out for an evening hunt and take the twelve-gauge. My little brother, who was two years younger than me, had pleaded with our dad to let him go with me. I hadn't considered this request and did not want him to go, as this was my first hunt with Dad's gun, and I wanted to do it alone. Dad, however, agreed that Randy could go. As disappointed as I was with this development, I wasn't going to let it hinder my first hunt with Dad's gun. As we were heading out, Dad stopped us and laid down the ground rules. I was to always be in front with the gun pointed out in front of us. Randy was to stay behind me and do as I said. We both agreed and headed off down the road toward Den's holler.

As soon as we were in the lane, Randy started trying to get me to agree to let him shoot the gun. I knew, however, if I did this and was found out, the gun would be taken away from me, and I could get a whipping from Dad as well. I repeatedly told Randy no and to get behind me. This seemed to enrage Randy, and I guess he decided to make it as hard for me as he could. All the way down the road to Den's holler, he stayed out in front of me. He just laughed and skipped, and I tried to insist he get behind me like Dad had instructed him to do. From the blacktop road we walked past Den's trailer and up the car path into the mouth of the holler. When we came to the path leading into the hunting spot, I stopped and waited for Randy to get behind me before I loaded the gun. After several minutes of taunting me, I guess he realized I wasn't going any farther until he got behind me. He finally slowly walked around me and stood behind me. I loaded the twelve-gauge and very proudly started my squirrel hunt.

When you squirrel hunt, you try to keep sound and motion as low and slow as possible, trying not to draw the attention of the squirrels. We started up the path, and immediately Randy started chattering about nothing, then ran around me to the front and was skipping and singing as loudly as he could. As we approached the point where several hickory nut trees stood and the squirrels were plentiful, I realized Randy was not going to let me hunt at all since I wouldn't let him shoot Dad's gun. This realization sent a bolt of anger through me like I had never had with my brother, and I started to scream at him. My face was red, my heart was pumping, and if he had been within arm's reach of me, I may have punched him.

My brother and I had fought as all boys do, especially brothers, but I had never felt so much anger toward him. I was standing there screaming profanities at him in this anger-fed state I was in. I suddenly realized he was smiling and laughing at me. He had never seen me this angry, and he was relishing the fact that he had brought me to this spot, that he had made me this angry. I stopped screaming and walked around him; he just stood there and let me go by. The next several minutes were quiet as I tried to hunt, although deep down inside, I knew the hunt was over. I walked a little farther up the path, and to my amazement, there was a squirrel. It was sitting out on a limb cutting a hickory nut. I motioned to Randy to stop, and I slowly raised the gun. The bang of the shotgun echoed through the holler as the squirrel jumped up to another limb and, in a flash, was gone. That's it, I thought as I broke down the shotgun and took out the spent shell. I walked back toward Randy as he began taunting me about missing. Then he went back to the same request of Let me shoot the gun. I walked past him and headed home. I wasn't going to listen to him anymore; I just wanted to get back to the house.

All the way down out of Den's holler, past his trailer. Randy was hounding me to shoot the gun. As we started up the blacktop road, I guess he knew I wasn't going to let him. So, he intensified his efforts, and now he was the one screaming and cussing at me. Dancing around me all the way up the road, he was getting more and more angry. He kept his barrage up as we came down the lane. As we walked and Randy was continuing his verbal attack on me, I seemed to find a calm place inside me that allowed me to just keep walking. I was hoping Dad would hear him and know what was going on so he wouldn't be allowed to go with me ever again, but that didn't happen. As we entered our yard, I continued walking and ignoring Randy. He, however, had reached a boiling point and was so mad that he was just calling me names and cussing me now in a quieter tone because Mom and Dad could hear us. Suddenly, I felt a thump on my back, like someone had punched me. I quickly realized that it was no punch as the burning sensation went through my back and into my arms. The pain was intense as. I fell to my knees and reached around to see what was causing this pain. Randy had thrown his squirrel pin at me, and it had stuck into my back. Just to the left of my spine, about halfway down my back. I could touch it, but I couldn't grasp it. Randy ran up to me as if to see what he had done.

"Pull it out" were the only words I could muster. Randy stood there for what seemed like several minutes before he yanked the pin out of my back and dropped it.

"Please don't tell," Randy pleaded as he ran into the house.

I turned and picked the squirrel pin up to look at it. It was bloody up about an inch. My brother had stabbed me, I thought as I raised myself up to walk into the house. In those moments, as I walked around the corner and into the house, I was debating with myself as to whether I was going to tell on Randy for stabbing me. I decided not to because he would get in so much trouble, and Dad would whip him hard. So, I went into the house and found Mom and Dad both sitting in the living room, where I would need to put the gun away. Dad kept old meat in the pot on the top hook of a gun rack I had made in junior high shop class. This meant I was going to need to raise both of my arms above my head with the gun to hang it up. I was in such pain simply holding the gun I wasn't sure if I could do it or not. Randy was in his bed, the lower bunk of our bunk beds, looking out into the living room as this all happened. Dad asked if I had gotten anything as I walked across the room to the gun rack. I explained how I had seen one but missed it. I slowly raised my arms to hang the gun on the rack. The pain was so intense I thought I was going to pass out, but I made it.

After the gun was secure, I went to the bathroom to see if I could see the wound. I could barely see the swollen welt where it went in. There was very little blood, I noticed, and that was a good thing because explaining a bloody spot on the back of my shirt was the last thing I wanted to do with our mom. I took some toilet paper and dabbed some of Dad's turpentine on it; this was what we used in those days as a disinfectant. I reached around as far as I could and swabbed the area as best I could. As I walked into our bedroom and went across to my bed, the top half of the bunk bed. I slowly sat down and looked—no, glared—at Randy. I wanted to yell at him, make him say he was sorry for what he had done. As I sat there staring at my brother, I realized the real reason I had not told on him. Somewhere in the back of my mind, I knew if I did tell on him or if either of my parents found out what had happened on this first hunt with the twelve gauge. I wouldn't be allowed to use it again for who knew how long. So, I sat there staring at my little brother with wave after wave of pain washing over me. Until the pain had eased enough for me to go on with my business. I was sore for the next few days, but all in all, I healed quickly. Though we have argued many times since that fateful evening in August, that was the only fight with my brother that ended in violence. I would never raise a hand in violence toward my brother under any circumstance, and I believe that he learned a lesson that day as well.

www.ingramcontent.com/pod-product-compliance
Lightning Source LLC
Chambersburg PA
CBHW061711120626
46550CB00003B/1182